SEARCHING

FOR

GOD

STUDY GUIDE

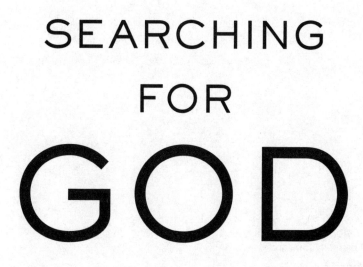

SEARCHING
FOR
GOD

IS THERE
ANY REASON TO BELIEVE
IN GOD TODAY?

STUDY GUIDE

HOLLY LAZZARO

ZONDERVAN
REFLECTIVE

ZONDERVAN REFLECTIVE

Searching for God Study Guide
Copyright © 2019 by Holly Lazzaro

ISBN 978-0-310-10779-8 (softcover)

ISBN 978-0-310-10780-4 (ebook)

Requests for information should be addressed to:
Zondervan, *3900 Sparks Dr. SE, Grand Rapids, Michigan 49546*

Cover design: Bruce Gore | Gore Studio, Inc.
Cover imagery: orestegaspari / iStockphoto
Interior design: Denise Froehlich

Printed in the United States of America

19 20 21 22 23 /LSC/ 10 9 8 7 6 5 4 3 2 1

CONTENTS

FOREWORD

Many in the church are caught off-guard by a range of objections to the Christian faith. This is a great pity because it isn't due to a lack of available resources. Indeed, in our day, we are sitting on a gold mine—both popular and scholarly—to assist Christians in working through their own individual questions and doubts as well as in the task of sharing their faith in Christ with others. The biblical faith can stand up to questions, and it makes better sense of the universe and of human experience than its alternatives. The *Searching for God* study helps make this point clearly and powerfully.

This study guide and video series is a valuable tool to equip Christians to think through their faith at a deeper level. It is my hope that churches, small groups, campus ministries, and others will make good use of this video and guide.

Paul Copan
Pledger Family Chair of Philosophy and Ethics
Palm Beach Atlantic University
coeditor of the *Dictionary of Christianity and Science* (Zondervan)

PREFACE

It all started after a three-month mission trip to Africa. I probably was on the highest spiritual mountaintop of my life. We had seen demons cast out of people, healings, and most importantly, many people come to Christ. When I came back to America, I wanted to share this life-changing experience with everyone. I told these stories to friends, family, and to strangers, and it was through my conversations with strangers that God began to plant the seeds in my heart that would later become *Searching for God*.

As I spoke with people in America, I noticed a consistent closed-mindedness to spiritual things. My stories were not taken seriously. At best, the response sounded something like, "Good for you, man; I'm glad you found something that works for you."

These conversations began to grow my curiosity about why people believe the things they do and, more specifically, what the core beliefs of an average American are. I wanted to know why the claims of Christianity seemed unbelievable or irrelevant to the people I talked with.

I started reaching out to Christian leaders and thinkers—people who would help me to better wrap my mind around the spiritual condition of the West and how we can best communicate the message of Christ to the world around us. I interviewed Paul Copan and Gary Habermas within the first month, and immediately they started shaping my understanding. I came to realize there are words to embody the belief systems I was encountering on the street. For example, when I told Dr. Copan the story I mentioned above, where I was told, "Good for you, man; I'm glad you found something that works for you," he explained that the person I had been speaking with was operating within a belief system called *relativism*. He explained what relativism is and why it is important for us as modern Christians to be aware of it. He also explained how we can expose its weaknesses and poke holes in its facade so that the light and truth of Christ might shine through to a person.

Over the period of a year, I continued to talk with people like William Lane Craig, Lee Strobel, Paul Copan, and many others. Through these interviews, my understanding of our times was sharpening. When it was time to edit the documentary, I had heard many of the same things repeated by the various speakers in the film. They helped to not only educate me personally but in fact provided most of the content, the story arc, and very much of the film itself. *Searching for God* is almost entirely the result of their education, inspiration, and hard work.

More recently, I connected with Holly Lazzaro from *Study with Friends*. Her commitment to the Word of God and her passion to expose more people to the message within *Searching for God* helped me realize what an important partnership this would be. Together, we have broken up the documentary into a six-unit study so that you can engage more deeply with the content of the film. Each unit features a 10-to-15-minute section of video and provides Scriptures to support the truths within the video as well as further insights and quotations from the scholars in the video. Each unit also features reflection questions to help you assess how to more effectively reach the lost with the new insights you gain through the videos. Our goal is that believers across America would be exposed to *Searching for God* not just to be entertained but also as a tool to be sharpened by, and that ultimately the information presented would be transformative both to individual churchgoers and to the people God has uniquely placed around them. We pray that *Searching for God* will lead to many fruitful conversations about Jesus, the many ways he is misrepresented in our culture, and the beautiful truth of who he actually is.

—Brandon McGuire, founder, *White Sail Films*. Director,
Searching for God documentary.

What an incredible journey this project has been. God worked in and through this project to grow me and show me himself and his great love for me and for you.

I started this project as a fervent believer in God's Word and a lover of apologetics. I have always enjoyed the way that apologetics remind me that thinkers do believe and believers do think. Coming from a family with many atheists, I was taught early to be a thinker. As I have walked my faith journey, I have held fast to my passion for the marriage of faith and intelligent thought. Contrary to popular belief, they really do marry well.

I am always excited about great apologetic works, because they edify and strengthen my faith. New ones always seem to come my way right on time, providing insight to a question that I am struggling with or new depth to an understanding I thought I had in hand. It is my hope that this project will do that for you.

I come alongside Brandon McGuire in this project honored, inspired, and humbled by the great thinkers who have contributed, and by Brandon's beautiful video work. Since Bible teaching is my passion, I have attempted to offer biblical resources to use as you process the information found in the videos. The filter of God's Word is how I have learned to process all things in my life. I offer that to you here.

As always, I lean on the miracle of the Holy Spirit to meet you where you are, providing you with greater wisdom than I could ever offer. I know that our Lord will reveal himself to you here, not because of anything I have written on a page, but because of what he wants to write upon your heart.

Holly

UNIT 1

THE STATE OF
CHRISTIANITY TODAY

VIDEO NOTES

"If you didn't know any real, serious, intelligent Christians, where would you come into contact with Christianity?"
DR. DONALD WILLIAMS

"You know, sometimes we use the same vocabulary but not the same dictionary, and I think that's really obvious when you start talking about things like morality and God and Christianity."
JOHN STONESTREET

CHAPTER 1

WHAT IS CHRISTIANITY?

The purpose of this study is to give you greater fluency in the Christian faith. The word "fluency" is used intentionally. If you are fluent in a language, you can speak it well. By the end of this study you will able to articulate what Christianity is, what it is not, and why it is so important.

We will explore together the ways that Christianity is viewed in American culture and discuss some of the ideas that compete with or contradict Christianity. By looking at the culture around us, we will understand how to engage friends and neighbors in conversations about faith in an informed, thoughtful, and loving way.

The main path we will take is a compare-and-contrast approach. The light for this path will, of course, be Scripture.

This study is designed to meet you wherever you are in your understanding of God, Jesus Christ, and the Christian faith. But the burden for that is not on the words in this book or on your ability to process them. It's on God. He promises to meet you where you are. In Jeremiah 33:3 he says, "Call to me and I will answer you and tell you great and unsearchable things you do not know." Let's decide here, right at the beginning, to let God do the heavy lifting. He can handle it. Pray before you start each unit of study. If you stumble over a certain term or idea, reflect on it and look at the resources provided for further clarification. And keep praying. Don't forget to invite God into the process of learning more about him! This is more than an intellectual exercise.

So, *What is Christianity?*

In the first video segment of *Searching for God*, you saw some illuminating interviews with ordinary Americans and their attempts to define Christianity. But maybe you wondered to yourself, "What would I say if I had been the man or woman on the street?" "Can I articulate my faith?" "Do I really have the answer to that question, 'What is Christianity?'"

Let's start, then, by creating common ground on that question. There's a reason why everyone loves John 3:16, so of course we will include that, but as we attempt to define what Christianity is, let's bookend that beloved Scripture with two others:

> All of us have become like one who is unclean, and all our righteous acts are like filthy rags; we all shrivel up like a leaf, and like the wind our sins sweep us away. (Isaiah 64:6)

> For God so loved the world that he gave his one and only Son, that whoever believes in him shall not perish but have eternal life. For God did not send his Son into the world to condemn the world, but to save the world through him. (John 3:16–17)

> God made him who had no sin to be sin for us, so that in him we might become the righteousness of God. (2 Corinthians 5:21)

If we take these three segments of Scripture and tie them into a brief description of the Christian faith, it's this:

1. Every human is born with deeply sinful, self-centered tendencies. We are unable to save ourselves and we are in need of a Savior.
2. God, our Creator and Father, in his love, mercy, and grace, provided the way for us to be rescued from sin—that is, the death and resurrection of his only Son Jesus Christ. Jesus Christ is fully man and fully God.
3. The Christian faith is all about the person of Jesus. The Christian is one who bears his name, follows his teaching, and accepts him as Savior and Lord.
4. Jesus Christ is the only provision for our sin. Accepting the free gift God gave us on the cross means trusting in Jesus, and trusting in Jesus means forgiveness and being reconciled to God. This is the only way to be with God when we die. It is also the only way to have a fulfilling, purposeful life here on earth.

This is not a complete, theologically nuanced definition. But it will serve as a simple, straightforward point from which we will start our journey together.

PERCEPTIONS OF CHRISTIANITY

"If you didn't know any real, serious, intelligent Christians, where would you come into contact with Christianity?"
DR. DONALD WILLIAMS

Now that we have established a few bedrock principles, let's explore the view of Christianity in our culture.

Imagine for a moment that you are entirely unfamiliar with Christianity. Where would you find information in the culture about Christianity?

....
....
....
....

If the only representation you have of Christianity is what you saw in the media, what would you "know" about Christianity?

....
....
....
....

How is Christianity portrayed in:

- *The Middle* (TV show)?

....
....
....
....

- *The Keepers* (Netflix)?

....
....
....
....

- *The DaVinci Code* (movie)?

....
....
....
....

List others:

....
....
....
....

"That's the image that, as far as the media is concerned, we present to the public. If that's all I knew about Christianity, I would have absolutely no interest in it."

DR. DONALD WILLIAMS

What are your greatest concerns about how people perceive Christianity in the culture?

....

....

....

....

Reflect on some of the things that people associate with Christianity:

- Christianity as one long list of rules or a religious system.

....

....

....

....

- Christians as white Protestant Westerners.

....

....

....

....

- Christians as extremists (intolerant, racist, hateful).

....

....

....

....

List others you can think of:

....

....

....

....

What are some other misperceptions that people have about Christianity?

....

....

....

....

What are the implications of these misperceptions?

....

....

....

....

Have you ever personally had any misperceptions about Christianity? How did you overcome them?

....

....

....

CHAPTER 3

HOW DO IDEAS BECOME "WORLDVIEWS"?

A worldview is a "philosophy of life"—that is, a comprehensive conception or apprehension of the world. This includes beliefs but also unconscious assumptions about what's real, what the good life is, what is right and wrong, whether we can know, whether life and history have purpose and meaning. And we can't forget that a personal heart commitment is at the root of every person's worldview.

A worldview is just what it sounds like: it's the way you view and make sense of the world. The word "worldview" has become popular recently because more and more people are interested in defining or getting clear on what their worldview is and how it compares with others. That's a good thing! That means the culture has become more interested in having these types of conversations.

How does an idea or concept become a worldview? We absorb assumptions, attitudes, and perspectives from our upbringing, our culture, our peers, our education. However, it's not as though we're helpless and can make no choices. We may consciously embrace much of what we grew up with, or rebel against it, or settle on an assortment of beliefs and attitudes.

Colleges and universities can have a big impact on our worldview. In a relatively short time, "higher ed" may not only challenge but wreck the beliefs of one's youth. Professors may challenge the Christian faith as uninformed—the stuff of weak intellects. Often, the only heresy on university campuses is orthodox Christianity. Such institutions clearly influence the worldview of their graduates.

A worldview is like the foundation of a house, which can't be seen but is necessary to keep the house standing. Or it is like a pair of lenses through which we see the world and make decisions accordingly. We ought to think through our philosophy of life to examine its foundations, to think about how we are viewing the world. It's possible to ask and even gradually change our worldview in light of the question: "Which worldview makes the best sense of the world around me and of human experience?" Even for the most intellectual and academic individual, a worldview is not a detached array of ideas. It is a deeply personal heart commitment. As such, it is not easily changed.

A *biblical* worldview starts with belief in Jesus Christ as the clear, authoritative revelation of God: "Anyone who has seen me has seen the Father" (John 14:9). We read of Jesus in the Scriptures, which are God's trustworthy revelation to us. Jesus is not only a historical figure but he also proves to be a trustworthy spiritual guide. The Scriptures aren't just "a nice book" or "an interesting collection of writings." To say that isn't holding to a biblical worldview.

Christians have discovered that the truth of Scripture offers foundational answers, and we can safely orient our lives around Christ and the priorities he sets for our lives. He becomes the foundation of everything we say and do.

Do you have a biblical worldview? Based on claims found in the Bible, the following questions were used by the Barna Research Group[1] in a nationwide survey:

- Do absolute moral truths exist?
- Is absolute truth defined by the Bible?
- Did Jesus Christ live a sinless life?
- Is God the all-powerful and all-knowing Creator of the universe, and does he still rule it today?
- Is salvation a gift from God that cannot be earned?
- Is Satan real?
- Does a Christian have a responsibility to share his or her faith in Christ with other people?
- Is the Bible accurate in all of its teachings?

Did you answer yes to these? Only 9 percent of self-titled Christians did.

The Bible teaches us about our worldview and reminds us that what we believe in our heart will inform everything we do:

---

1   Research Releases in Faith and Christianity (August 2005), www.barna.com/research/most-adults-feel-accepted-by-god-but-lack-a-biblical-worldview/.

Above all else, guard your heart, for everything you do flows from it. (Proverbs 4:23)

What are some worldviews that come to your mind?

....

....

....

....

Have you ever thought about your worldview before?

....

....

....

....

What is your worldview as you start this class? Can you articulate that worldview? If you were asked on the street, "What is the Christian faith?" what would you say?

....

....

....

....

Are there questions you have about Christianity and the Christian worldview?

....

....

....

CHAPTER 4

WORDS MATTER

When using language, you display an understanding of how to use the words of that language in communication with others. This is a complex process that we often take for granted in everyday conversations. John Stonestreet reminds us to look at our understanding of the words we use a little more carefully as we engage friends and family about our faith:

> "You know, sometimes we use the same vocabulary but not the same dictionary, and I think that's really obvious when you start to talk about things like morality and God and Christianity."

Reflect on the cultural definition of the following words, and contrast them with the Christian definition of those words. This will highlight how we can "use the same [words] but not the same dictionary." For help on the Christian definition of each, see the Scriptures noted.

LOVE

> Greater love has no one than this, that someone lay down his life for his friends. (John 15:13 ESV)

Cultural definition of love:

....

....

....

....

Faith

Now faith is the assurance of things hoped for, the conviction of things not seen. For by it the people of old received their commendation. By faith we understand that the universe was created by the word of God, so that what is seen was not made out of things that are visible. (Hebrews 11:1–3 ESV)

Now Jesus did many other signs in the presence of the disciples, which are not written in this book; but these are written so that you may believe [i.e., have faith] that Jesus is the Christ, the Son of God, and that by believing you may have life in his name. (John 20:30–31 ESV)

Cultural definition of faith:

....

....

....

....

Success

This Book of the Law shall not depart from your mouth, but you shall meditate on it day and night, so that you may be careful to do according to all that is written in it. For then you will make your way prosperous, and then you will have good success. (Joshua 1:8 ESV)

Cultural definition of success:

....

....

....

....

What are some other words that have different meanings for Christians and non-Christians?

....

....

....

CHAPTER 5

CULTURAL CHRISTIANITY

In his message to the 2006 Desiring God National Conference, Tim Keller said:

"[America is] perhaps the most challenging mission field yet, because no one [has] ever had to evangelize on a large scale a society that used to be Christian. Certainly there have been many times in the past when the church was in serious decline, and revival revitalized the faith and society. But in those times society was still nominally Christian. There hadn't been a wholesale erosion of the very concepts of God and truth and of the basic reliability and wisdom of the Bible. Things are different now.

"Inoculation introduces a mild form of a disease into a body, thereby stimulating the growth of antibodies and rendering the person immune to getting a full-blown version of the sickness. In the same way, post-Christian society contains unique resistance and 'antibodies' against full-blown Christianity. For example, the memory of sustained injustices that flourished under more Christianized Western societies has become an antibody against the gospel. Christianity was big back when blacks had to sit on [sic] the back of the bus and when women were beaten up by men without consequences. We've tried out a Christian society and it wasn't so hot. Been there. Done that."[1]

---

1   "The Supremacy of Christ and the Gospel in a Postmodern World," Desiring God, 2006 Desiring God National Conference, www.desiringgod.org/messages/the-supremacy-of-christ-and-the-gospel-in-a-postmodern-world (emphasis removed).

Do you agree or disagree that modern-day America has been "inoculated" by Christianity? If so, what are some ways that we Americans have been inoculated, and how do you think this "inoculation" plays out in current culture?

....

....

....

....

> A lot of people tend to think of themselves as being Christian simply because they're born in America and this is kind of a Christian culture. . . . What's interesting is that oftentimes when you talk to people in the United States who might identify as Christians, it turns out that they're nominal Christians, or they're cultural Christians. In other words, they've bought into the cultural trappings of Christianity but when you press them upon morality and how they should live, or about the nature of theology—about the trinity, or the death and resurrection of Jesus Christ—they tend to not know how to answer those questions because it turns out they're actually not that churched. They don't attend services regularly. They don't know much about Christianity. And so you have this large population of people who turn out to be nominally Christian, in name only.
>
> ALAN SHLEMON

What does it look like to be "nominally Christian, in name only"? How does that life differ from a life fully embracing the Christian worldview?

....

....

....

....

In a world that misrepresents Christianity so severely, what can we do to lovingly correct mistaken interpretations? Please don't miss the focus on *lovingly*.

....

....

....

....

How might we respond *in love* to those who have encountered only false expressions of our faith?

....

....

....

....

Do you think it's easy to slip out of loving, gentle conversation into arguments about faith and mistaken interpretations or expressions of the Christian faith? If so, what do you think is the cause of that shift in us, and how do we overcome it?

....

....

....

....

Make a short list of people in your life who don't share your Christian worldview. We will come back to this list later with practical resources you can use to engage them in loving conversation. For now, be intentional about praying for them each day. Ask God to show them evidence of himself in your life, and ask him to show you opportunities to share your faith, with or without words.

....

....

....

....

....

UNIT 2

THE THEORY OF NATURALISM

VIDEO NOTES

"In order to understand how Christianity is currently viewed in America, I would need to look at what other ideas have been accepted by our culture. I wanted to know what ideas have led to this confusion about Christianity and made the claims of Christianity seem unbelievable."

BRANDON MCGUIRE

"It seems to me that among the principle ideas competing with Christian theism today would be naturalism: the view that only the natural world exists, that there are no supernatural entities, and that knowledge and truth is to be found exclusively through science alone. I think naturalism deeply permeates Western culture."

WILLIAM LANE CRAIG

"The dominant story that explains the world for most modern people in the West now is [naturalistic] evolution. We are the product of blind purposeless forces operating purely by chance, and we are essentially therefore no different from the rest of creation. We're no different from the animals except we have maybe a couple of extra convolutions in our brains and opposable thumbs."

DR. DONALD WILLIAMS

NATURALISM

In our first unit, we looked at the state of Christianity in America today. We saw how the Christian faith is perceived by, and in some ways interacts with, American culture. This unit will begin to tackle some different ideas that conflict with or contradict the Christian faith.

Sometimes reading about concepts like naturalism, relativism, and pluralism will feel like trying to drink water from a fire hose. That's okay. The idea of this study is to help you understand these theories and to be informed by them in your own faith walk and in your conversations with the people around you.

There is a glossary in the back of this book to help you understand the terms that might be new to you. Read the definitions, take in what you can, and do your best to think through the key concepts being absorbed by many in our society. Although you may not use the terms "naturalism" or "religious pluralism" in ordinary conversation, by the end of this study you should understand those ideas more clearly and be able to translate that understanding into your everyday interactions with the Bible, with other Christians, and with nonbelievers.

With that in mind, let's get started.

CHAPTER 6

WHAT IS NATURALISM?

*N*aturalism is like a three-legged stool: one has to do with *reality* ("**metaphysics**"), another with *causes* ("**etiology**"), and the third with *knowledge* ("**epistemology**"). Let's spell that out by referring to three "isms":

Materialism: All reality is physical. There is no God, no soul, no afterlife, no angelic beings. For many naturalists, even consciousness (or mental awareness) is an illusion since it's not physical.

Determinism: Every event is completely predictable because it is produced by prior causes and effects going all the way back to the Big Bang. This includes our thoughts, which means there is no personal responsibility or free will. A determinist believes we're helpless and can't help doing what we do. Because every event has a logical, predictable cause, the determinist also rules out the miraculous—such as Jesus's turning water into wine or being raised from the dead.

Scientism: Science is the only (or best) way to obtain knowledge. If you can't scientifically prove it, it's not knowable.

Materialism, determinism, and scientism summarize the heart of strict naturalism. Ideas that stem from naturalism:

Metaphysical Naturalism: Nature is all that exists; all things supernatural therefore do not exist.

Methodological Naturalism: Observable events in nature are explained only by natural causes; the scientific method (hypothesize, predict, test, repeat) is the only effective way to investigate reality.

Broad Naturalism: Some naturalists reject strict naturalism because of its stark implications. These individuals embrace a "naturalism-plus," which includes the reality of consciousness, human dignity, moral duties, personal responsibility, beauty, and so on. In this case, however, their worldview "house" has moved in a lot of furniture from the house of the biblical faith. It looks a lot more like *theism* than naturalism.

"[Naturalism is] the view that only the natural world exists, that there are no supernatural entities, and that knowledge and truth is to be found exclusively through science alone. . . . Naturalism deeply permeates Western culture."

WILLIAM LANE CRAIG

The theory of naturalism rejects God because God is immaterial and independent of nature and not subject to natural laws and processes. Many scientists live and breathe the visible, observable universe; that is, they assume the universe is all of reality. God doesn't fit their worldview. Anything that might be attributable to God—the beginning or fine-tuning of the universe, say—must have a naturalistic explanation.

CHAPTER 7

CREATION

Naturalism conflicts with Christianity on many important levels. However, the Christian's disagreement with naturalism does not have to equate to personal conflict with naturalists. As believers, we can (and should) have good, loving relationships with individuals who hold many different points of view. The Bible reminds us of that in Colossians 4:5–6:

> Be wise in the way you act toward outsiders; make the most of every opportunity. Let your conversation be always full of grace, seasoned with salt, so that you may know how to answer everyone.

The Christian's dispute with naturalism is a simple disagreement about the existence of God, who is independent of nature—indeed, the very source of the natural world itself. Creation provides a good platform to highlight the contrast. So, given our assumption that our conversations must be characterized by love, let's look at how naturalism views origins.

Many modern naturalists acknowledge **the Big Bang theory** as the best description of the universe's beginning, and they view undesigned evolution as the explanation for life afterward. The Big Bang theory states the universe originated 13.8 billion years ago in an explosion from a single point of nearly infinite energy density. At that time, the entire universe was inside a bubble that was thousands of times smaller than a pinhead. It was hotter and denser than anything we can imagine. Then it suddenly exploded. The universe that we know was born. Time, space, and matter all began with the Big Bang. In a fraction of a second, the universe grew from smaller than a single atom to bigger than a galaxy. And it kept on growing at a fantastic rate. It is still expanding today.

Long before scientists conceived of the Big Bang theory, medieval Jewish, Christian, and Muslim philosophers reasoned that the past series of events couldn't be infinite. The past had a beginning and thus must have had a cause.

Looking at things from another angle, the seventeenth-century philosopher G. W. Leibniz asked, "Why is there something rather than nothing at all?" Either something exists because it depends on something outside of itself (i.e., it is contingent) or by virtue of its own nature (i.e., it is self-existent). Clearly, the universe is contingent. According to the second law of thermodynamics, all energy tends toward dissipation or spreading out; the universe is winding down, which means that it has been wound up. The principle "from nothing nothing comes" has been a mainstay in science. If the universe began to exist, something already existing brought it about. Yet some modern scientists and philosophers ignore or bypass the evidence that points to God or a creator. For example, in a radio program aired on BBC in 1948, Bertrand Russell, an agnostic famous for debating science and religion, says, "The universe is just there. And that's all."[1]

The Christian perspective of creation by God is found in the Genesis chapter 1 narrative. Genesis 1:1, which John 1:1–3 echoes, points to an absolute beginning—creation out of nothing. This is followed by a literary and theological picture of three divisions on the first three days which create various spheres or "forms" (1: day/night; 2: waters above/waters beneath; 3: land/waters). Then in the next three days, those forms are "filled" (4: the sun, moon, and stars; 5: the birds of the air and the fish of the sea; 6: land animals and humans). Perhaps open a Bible and take a moment to read Genesis 1.

Is the creation of the universe an important question for Christians to discuss with each other? With nonbelievers? Why or why not?

....

....

....

---

1 "Father Copleston vs. Bertrand Russell: The Famous 1948 BBC Radio Debate on the Existence of God." www.biblicalcatholic .com/apologetics/p20.htm.

CHAPTER 8

EVOLUTION AND INTELLIGENT DESIGN

The theory of **evolution** was popularly established by Charles Darwin (1809–1882). Modern naturalists say that evolution defines how the variety of living organisms have developed from a common ancestor (i.e., all organisms are related) and diversified from earlier forms during the history of the earth. For example, reptiles transformed into birds and apes transformed into humans.

The *theory* of evolution has been adopted as *fact* by many modern scientists who believe that all life evolved from a single common source. However, Darwin himself did not propose this. The title of Darwin's most famous book is often given incorrectly as *The Origin of the Species*, as if it were about the origin of our species. But the title is actually *On the Origin of Species*—meaning "where do species come from?" The short answer provided in the book is that species are descended from common ancestors, winnowed by natural selection and not independently created. Darwin's book is about the general process of the evolution of *each* species. It does not trace the origin of any particular species, including humans. (The longish subtitle to the book is: *By Means of Natural Selection, Or, the Preservation of Favoured Races in the Struggle for Life.*)

Natural selection, mentioned in that subtitle, is the process whereby organisms better adapted to their environment tend to survive and produce more offspring. Since there is competition for limited resources available between organisms, the only traits that are passed on are the strong traits.

The Age of Reason (circa 1685–1815, just coming to a close as Darwin was born) influenced the events that followed this historical theory. The Age of Reason radically reoriented philosophy and science, as you might guess, away from traditional religion and toward *reason*, logic, and evidence. Skepticism was a virtue in this age, and that thinking has persisted. The groundwork for this thinking was set by Descartes, Locke, and Spinoza and reinforced by

David Hume and Immanuel Kant. Generally speaking, this era shifts the cultural conversation from what we believe to what we can prove, effectively boxing out God. This continues to be the rub between scientists and theologians today: Is God provable?

What is often forgotten or even suppressed about Darwin and his theory is that he indicated his own balance of thought between science and faith, ***specifically in the context of evolutionary theory***. Toward the end of the book, he speaks of "laws impressed on matter by the Creator" and of life "having been originally breathed by the Creator into a few forms or into one . . . from so simple a beginning endless forms most beautiful and most wonderful have been, and are being evolved." This balanced thinking seems to be anathema in the community of evolutionary theorists today.

While Christians themselves disagree about the evolution question, Christian philosopher Alvin Plantinga has said that the crux of the matter is guided vs. unguided evolution—God vs. no God. The matter of direct vs. indirect creation is secondary; it's not logically impossible that God could have used the evolutionary process to bring about his purposes. Many Christians believe that these two—a designing God and the process of evolution—dovetail nicely. That's a discussion for another day. But if we are simply products of mindless, unguided processes, we must deny the biblical truth that we humans have been "fearfully and wonderfully made" (Psalm 139:14). The believer will have to affirm ***intelligent design***—the idea that the universe and life itself cannot have arisen by chance and was designed and created by some intelligent entity.

If one believes that humans evolved in an utterly unguided naturalistic process from single-celled organisms, one is excluding the possibility that humans were created by an Intelligent Designer—God. These processes are either the product of a designing mind or they are not. Naturalism and theism box each other out. This is called **mutual exclusivity**. You can't believe both truth claims at the same time. While both theories could be false, both cannot be true. We will talk more about mutual exclusivity in unit 3 when we look at different truth claims across religions.

What are some examples of mutual exclusivity from everyday life?

....

....

....

....

There are many layers of complexity surrounding the theory of evolution. One problem is that the culture has apprehended an understanding of this theory that is quite different from Darwin's original intention. We attribute some ideas to Darwin that he did not explicitly propose or endorse.

Darwin himself did not coin the phrase "survival of the fittest," though it is often credited to him. This is an expression developed by Herbert Spencer (1820–1903) to apply an extension of Darwin's theory to the social realm. Spencer's **social Darwinism** is the theory that human groups and races are subject to the same laws of natural selection as Charles Darwin had perceived in plants and animals in nature. This theory offers some intriguing insights into the human social condition. Darwin knew about some of the troubling ethical implications of naturalistic (and social) Darwinism in his day, but he didn't comment on them. Yet many in our culture blindly accept some of these problematic moral conclusions, including humans being "nothing more than animals" or that morality is just a "corporate illusion fobbed off on us by our genes to get us to cooperate."[1]

In the video, Lee Strobel reminds us:

> Whenever we see information, there is always an intelligence behind it. Nature can't produce information. It can produce patterns. So if you're walking down the beach and you see ripples in the wet sand you would say, 'Okay, the wave action or the tide action caused the ripples to be created, because nature can create patterns. But if you're walking down the beach and you see "John loves Mary" in the sand, and a heart around it and an arrow through it, you would never say, "The waves did that!" Why? Because it's information. Whenever we see information, whether it's a book, a software code, a painting on a cave wall . . . wherever we see information, we know there's intelligence behind it. Well, if that's true, what about the vast storehouse of information inside every one of the cells in your body?

---

1   Michael Ruse and E. O. Wilson, "The Evolution of Ethics," in *Religion and the Natural Sciences*, ed. J. E. Huchingson (Orlando: Harcourt Brace, 1993), 310–11. For discussion on this, see Matthew H. Nitecki and Doris V. Nitecki, *Evolutionary Ethics* (Albany: State University of New York Press, 1993), 8.

The Bible teaches us very clearly that we were made, and made in God's image.

> So God created mankind in his own image, in the image of God he created them; male and female he created them. (Genesis 1:27)

The Bible goes on to tell us that all of creation declares God's name.

> For since the creation of the world God's invisible qualities—his eternal power and divine nature—have been clearly seen, being understood from what has been made, so that people are without excuse. (Romans 1:20)

What are the created things that make you most aware of God's hand? A sunset? The complexity of the human body? The pattern on a leaf or snowflake? Take some time to worship our Creator by listing the ways you see the design of his hand around you.

....

....

....

....

Why do you think that some people can't (or won't) see God in creation? How can you start a conversation about creation and God in a loving, nonconfrontational way by using examples from your list above?

....

....

....

CHAPTER 9

BODIES AND SOULS

We humans are embodied selves. Your self is your soul—it is who you are. One's "soul" is who that person is. I am a soul, and my soul can survive without a body after death—even though this is a state of incompleteness. Our souls will be joined to our bodies, which will be raised immortal—a "transformed physicality" as one scholar puts it (cf. Romans 8:23; Philippians 3:21; 1 Corinthians 15:53–54). As we consider the natural vs. the supernatural, let's also consider our bodies and our souls. Michael Sherrard reminds us:

> "I refer to my body as a possession. A possession of what? What's possessing my body? Why do we use language like that? We just know there are immaterial things. People understand there are souls, even if we can't articulate it, describe accurately or understand fully what a soul is—we know we have souls."

Read 1 Corinthians 6:19–20 and reflect on the body and soul relationship:

> Do you not know that your bodies are temples of the Holy Spirit, who is in you, whom you have received from God? You are not your own; you were bought at a price. Therefore honor God with your bodies.

....
....
....
....

Read the following passages and consider how they inform our understanding of bodies and souls. What do they tell you?

> But the other criminal rebuked him. "Don't you fear God," he said, "since you are under the same sentence? We are punished justly, for we are getting what our deeds deserve. But this man has done nothing wrong."
>
> Then he said, "Jesus, remember me when you come into your kingdom."
>
> Jesus answered him, "Truly I tell you, today you will be with me in paradise." (Luke 23:40–43)

> Jesus said to her, "I am the resurrection and the life. The one who believes in me will live, even though they die." (John 11:25)

> "Very truly I tell you, whoever obeys my word will never see death." (John 8:51)

> I am torn between the two: I desire to depart and be with Christ, which is better by far; but it is more necessary for you that I remain in the body. (Philippians 1:23–24)

> Because when we are clothed, we will not be found naked. For while we are in this tent, we groan and are burdened, because we do not wish to be unclothed but to be clothed instead with our heavenly dwelling, so that what is mortal may be swallowed up by life. Now the one who has fashioned us for this very purpose is God, who has given us the Spirit as a deposit, guaranteeing what is to come.
>
> Therefore we are always confident and know that as long as we are at home in the body we are away from the Lord. For we live by faith, not by sight. We are confident, I say, and would prefer to be away from the body and at home with the Lord. (2 Corinthians 5:3–8)

But you have come to Mount Zion, to the city of the living God, the heavenly Jerusalem. You have come to thousands upon thousands of angels in joyful assembly. (Hebrews 12:22)

....

....

....

....

What do you believe about the body-soul relationship?

....

....

....

CHAPTER 10

MIRACLES

Another place we can contrast Christian belief with naturalism is in the existence of miracles.

For the naturalist's perspective on miracles, let's go to an individual who planted his flag in this particular issue, the Scottish skeptic David Hume (1711–1776).

Hume claims that miracles are simply incredible. He starts his attack on miracles with the comment, "I flatter myself that I have discovered an argument . . . which, if just, will, with the wise and learned, be an everlasting check to all kinds of superstitious delusion, and consequently will be useful as long as the world endures."[1]

Hume's argument can be abbreviated:

1. A miracle is a violation of the laws of nature.
2. Firm and unalterable experience has established these laws of nature.
3. A wise person measures belief to evidence.
4. Therefore, the proof against miracles is overwhelming.

Consider the circular nature of Hume's argument:

If this is his argument, then it clearly defines miracles as impossible. For if miracles are a "violation" of what cannot be "altered," then miracles are impossible.

A person of faith could avoid this dilemma. He or she could refuse to define miracles as "violations" of fixed law and simply call them "exceptions" to a rule. It's like a professor

miracles can't happen

miracles violate natural laws

we should only believe what we can measure

evidence is measured via natural law

---

1 David Hume, *An Enquiry Concerning Human Understanding*, 10.1.18.

canceling a class; this doesn't mean that the entire university can no longer function in an orderly fashion. We could add that the beginning of the universe (the Big Bang) could be considered the first miracle; if all matter, energy, space, and time were produced from nothing by God, then why would turning water into wine or being raised from the dead be a problem?

This is an oversimplification of both Hume's theory and the Christian response. However, for the purpose of this course, it's adequate. Hume shows us a position that a naturalist might take on the idea of miracles, and we have shown there are responses that a believer might support.

What does God's Word have to say about miracles?

First, that they do occur. There are many references to miracles in both the Old and New Testaments. Second and just as important, miracles are not random. Rather, God always uses miracles for his own glory and to bring people into relationship with himself.

With that understanding, we might see miracles as a tender mercy, a gift from God to show himself to us.

> The Lord is not slow in keeping his promise, as some understand slowness. Instead he is patient with you, not wanting anyone to perish, but everyone to come to repentance. (2 Peter 3:9)

Read through the verses below. Note your thoughts on what they show about God's use of miracles.

> When the Israelites saw the mighty hand of the Lord displayed against the Egyptians, the people feared the Lord and put their trust in him and in Moses his servant. (Exodus 14:31)

....

....

....

....

You are the God who performs miracles; you display your power among the peoples. (Psalm 77:14)

....
....
....
....

"Unless you people see signs and wonders," Jesus told him, "you will never believe." (John 4:48)

....
....
....
....

When he heard this, Jesus said, "This sickness will not end in death. No, it is for God's glory so that God's Son may be glorified through it." (John 11:4)

....
....
....
....

Jesus performed many other signs in the presence of his disciples, which are not recorded in this book. But these are written that you may believe that Jesus is the Messiah, the Son of God, and that by believing you may have life in his name. (John 20:30–31)

....
....
....

THE CULTURAL IMPACT OF NATURALISM

Naturalism is a popular American worldview that is in direct conflict with the Christian worldview. If we want to engage the culture around us, it's important to understand the naturalistic perspective. As you grow to understand naturalism, you may find that this theory has had an influence on the worldview of many Christians. This is an even greater reason for Christians to understand it.

To review, the theory of naturalism says:

1. There is no God and no supernatural.
2. What we see in our world today is the result of time and chance and the laws of nature working on matter.
3. Miracles are not possible because they are a violation of the laws of nature.
4. If nonmaterial things such as consciousness, morality, logic, and personhood exist, naturalism reduces them to products of material causes.

With this theory in place, other beliefs follow:

1. There is no purpose or meaning to life—we are simply the product of time and chance and the laws of nature.
2. There are no moral truths or duties that apply to all people in all times; moral values are simply personal beliefs or opinions, which are the result of chemical and physical processes to enhance survival and reproduction.
3. There is no life after death, for the laws of nature still apply and our bodies simply decay over time and are mixed in with other nonliving matter in the earth.

Looking at the lists above, make some notes about how Christianity offers a different hope, point by point.

....

....

....

....

William Provine, an atheist and professor of biology at Cornell University, put his naturalistic view this way:

> Let me summarize my views on what modern evolutionary biology tells us loud and clear—and these are basically Darwin's views. There are no gods, no purposes, no goal-directed forces of any kind. There is no life after death. When I die, I am absolutely certain that I am going to be dead. That's the end for me. There is no ultimate foundation for ethics, no ultimate meaning to life, and no free will for humans, either.[1]

Famous atheist Richard Dawkins expressed a similar view:

> The universe we observe has precisely the properties we should expect if there is at bottom no design, no purpose, no evil and no good. Nothing but blind, pitiless indifference. DNA neither knows nor cares. DNA just is, and we dance to its music.[2]

Since naturalism teaches there is no higher authority (no God), it concludes that mankind, creation, and individuals have no purpose in life. With its insistence that there is no soul, no mind, and no self, naturalism also teaches that there is no choice. Every impulse we have, every action we take, every word we say is determined by the events that came before.

God understands how our environment can influence our actions. We see evidence of this through Scriptures that encourage us to meditate on his Word.

---

1   William Provine, "Darwinism: Science or Naturalistic Philosophy?," *Origins Research* 16.1–2 (1994): 9.
2   Richard Dawkins, *River Out of Eden* (New York: Basic, 1995), 133.

You shall therefore lay up these words of mine in your heart and in your soul, and you shall bind them as a sign on your hand, and they shall be as frontlets between your eyes. (Deuteronomy 11:18 ESV)

Set your minds on things that are above, not on things that are on earth. (Colossians 3:2 ESV)

How do these verses help us understand our environment's influence on our actions?

....

....

....

....

God reminds us that mankind has a specific purpose, contradicting the naturalist belief that life has no purpose, we only exist and then we don't. Here are a few purposes that God has given us:

The purpose of joining God as **co-regents** in caring for the earth:

Then God said, "Let us make mankind in our image, in our likeness, so that they may rule over the fish in the sea and the birds in the sky, over the livestock and all the wild animals, and over all the creatures that move along the ground."

So God created mankind in his own image, in the image of God he created them; male and female he created them.

God blessed them and said to them, "Be fruitful and increase in number; fill the earth and subdue it. Rule over the fish in the sea and the birds in the sky and over every living creature that moves on the ground." (Genesis 1:26–28)

The purpose of showing his glory and power and sharing in the divine life of the Trinity:

> But I have raised you up for this very purpose, that I might show you my power and that my name might be proclaimed in all the earth. (Exodus 9:16)

> This is eternal life: that they know you, the only true God, and Jesus Christ, whom you have sent. (John 17:3)

> He has saved us and called us to a holy life—not because of anything we have done but because of his own purpose and grace. (2 Timothy 1:9)

NOTE: Scripture speaks of "the fool [who] says in his heart, 'There is no God'" (Psalm 14:1). The point is not so much atheism as it is a belief that God is removed and unconcerned and won't hold me to account. After all, in Psalm 10, the one who in his thoughts has "no room for God" (v. 4) claims, "God will never notice; he covers his face and never sees" (v. 11). He "revile[s] God" and says to himself, "[God] won't call me to account" (v. 13).

What are some ways that naturalism has affected American culture?

....

....

....

....

Review the definition of naturalism (there is a glossary in the back of this book for reference). What are some ways that naturalism would affect the decision-making process of an individual or society that holds this worldview? In contrast, how does the Christian worldview impact the decision-making process of an individual or society?

....

....

....

....

Do you know anyone who embraces the ideas of naturalism? What snags have you encountered (or would you expect to encounter) in a conversation as it relates to your faith?

....

....

....

....

How can we build a bridge of communication with someone who holds a naturalist worldview?

....

....

....

....

Do you think that naturalism has influenced you in ways you didn't understand before? Explain.

....

....

....

CHAPTER 12

PROBLEMS WITH THE NATURALISTIC THEORY

There are three issues with naturalism. Let's take a look at these in turn.

1. Naturalism defies common sense and undercuts our very humanity. For example, some naturalists believe that consciousness (awareness) is an illusion. But to experience an illusion requires consciousness! Some naturalists believe that morality is a product of evolution that enhances survival and reproduction. Do these individuals believe in human rights and human dignity and moral duties? Is evil itself just an illusion? And what about our deepest longings? Don't we need forgiveness and guilt removal for wrongs done? What about our longing for significance and security? If a theory discards these basic features of reality and human experience, then the *theory* must go, not the inescapable reality of our experience.

2. Nature itself began to exist a finite time ago. If everything that begins to exist has a cause, then the universe's (or nature's) beginning has a cause that existed independent of it. Bertrand Russell's "The universe is just there. And that's all" is a false claim. The universe began to exist, and God makes the best sense of this. By rejecting God as the cause of the universe, the naturalist has nowhere to land for a beginning.

Some may reply, "But who made God?" This reply actually assumes atheism (i.e., it is question begging). The **theist** doesn't claim that everything that exists has a cause—only that everything that *begins* to exist has a cause. By his very nature, God necessarily exists; the universe doesn't since it is contingent. In fact, unless something can pop into existence, uncaused, out of nothing (which is metaphysically impossible), then we're inescapably left with something that has always been there.

3. The theory of naturalism backfires on itself. If nature is all that exists, and everything is the result of time and chance and the laws of nature, then the naturalist or atheist cannot trust that his own thoughts are true. If the naturalist's thoughts are the result of chemical and physical processes operating in his brain, then his beliefs are just accidental beliefs over which he has no control. The same would be true for the theist's beliefs, which would also be products of those same blind, deterministic processes. Neither can help believing what he does, and there's no way we can know who is right since we don't have control of those chemically induced beliefs. The naturalist has no way to explain the laws of nature that he relies on to understand the world. In fact, if he claims he truly *knows* something, the naturalist must borrow from the biblical worldview, which offers an excellent context for rationality and knowledge.

Do you think science and faith in God contradict each other or complement each other? Why?

....

....

....

COMPASSIONATE CONVERSATIONS

Let's try to return in each chapter to the core purpose of this study: to equip you with better understanding of your faith—that's first and foremost. Exploring the ideas that contradict Christianity should give us a deeper understanding of our faith.

You may find that as you gain that deeper understanding, you are excited to share it with people around you. It's important to lead those conversations with *love*. If you go into a conversation with the intent of winning an argument, you just might win that argument! But you probably won't win that heart.

Read Ephesians 4:11–16:

> Christ himself gave the apostles, the prophets, the evangelists, the pastors and teachers, to equip his people for works of service, so that the body of Christ may be built up until we all reach unity in the faith and in the knowledge of the Son of God and become mature, attaining to the whole measure of the fullness of Christ. Then we will no longer be infants, tossed back and forth by the waves, and blown here and there by every wind of teaching and by the cunning and craftiness of people in their deceitful scheming. Instead, speaking the truth in love, we will grow to become in every respect the mature body of him who is the head, that is, Christ. From him the whole body, joined and held together by every supporting ligament, grows and builds itself up in love, as each part does its work.

Informed and encouraged by these verses, write down some ideas on how we can speak to a friend who has a naturalistic point of view.

....

....

....

....

....

....

Make a short list of people in your life who might hold the naturalistic worldview. We will come back to this list later with practical resources you can use to engage them in loving conversation. For now, pray for them each day. Ask God to show them evidence of himself in your life, and ask him to show you opportunities to share your faith, with or without words.

....

....

....

....

THE THEORY OF RELATIVISM

VIDEO NOTES

"More often than not, people are resistant to the rule of God in their lives. I think that's why relativism is so dominant. People say, 'That's true for you but not for me.' They're not relativist when it comes to what the capital of France is, Paris. They're not relativist when it comes to who won the Super Bowl this past year. They're not relativist when it comes to what the stock numbers are. They're relativist when it comes to God, and they're relativist when it comes to morality."

PAUL COPAN

"People say, 'Yeah, I'm spiritual. I believe in some kind of god. That's good enough. That's fine.' When that's kind of meaningless. If you believe in just any god, that means you really believe in nothing."

LEE STROBEL

"I think the problem is in our culture, for the most part. People have adopted, 'Anything close is good enough.' That kind of an attitude. You see it on bumper stickers, you know, where you see people are trying to say, 'Can't we all get along?' . . . 'Tolerance.' You know, or how people will write the bumper stickers that kind of make the claim that 'all religions are the same. . . . Can't we just all get along with each other? They all are so close to the same, there's no point in arguing about it.' That's kind of the claim of the culture."

J. WARNER WALLACE

"Many people . . . advance the idea known as religious pluralism. Now they don't say that term, but this is in essence what it means: they think that all religions are basically the same."

ALAN SHLEMON

RELATIVISM

In our previous units together, we have been tossing around some ideas that permeate American culture. From misperceptions about Christianity to theories that are in direct conflict with what the Bible teaches us, we have made some good headway into better understanding our own worldview and the worldviews that exist around us.

Remember to take in this information at a rate that you can process it. Don't be frustrated if not all of it is sticking. The mind is like a muscle, and the more we exercise it, the better we'll become at using it. The good news is the written word will stick around as long as you keep it out of the recycle bin and you keep reviewing it. You can come back to the terms and the theories at your own pace and as God leads you. Trust that as you devote this time to understanding him better, he will be faithful to bring fruit from that process.

CHAPTER 13

WHAT IS RELATIVISM?

Relativism is (a) a theory that knowledge is *relative* to the limited nature of the mind and the conditions of knowing, and (b) a view that ethical truths depend on the individuals and groups holding them. The first relates to *truth*, the second to *morality*.

When it comes to traditional religious beliefs, *religious* relativism affirms that faith is relative to one's upbringing, culture, or geographical location. One's Buddhist or Taoist belief may even be a matter of personal preference. "Faith" (however one defines it) is a function of culture or personal preference. Whether it's truth, morality, or religion, what's right or good depends entirely on what is accepted by those around you or what you choose: "This is just right for me, but not necessarily for you." Relativism is the absence of an absolute.

What are some other ideas that are relative? What are some ideas that are NOT relative?

....
....
....
....

EXAMPLES OF RELATIVISM

Some ideas that stem from relativism follow. These are commonly heard and said in our culture:

"That's just your truth."
"We should be accepting of all beliefs."

56

"It's arrogant to say that your views are true for everyone."

"You shouldn't judge someone else's beliefs."

"Who are you to impose your morality on others?"

"You can do whatever you want—just as long as you don't hurt anyone."

Let's briefly examine these relativistic claims. Following are some good answers to these tough challenges. However, as Christians we must remember to be *loving first* and to package intelligent responses in a Christ-honoring way.

Every person you encounter is an image-bearer of God. Every. Single. One. So be careful that you don't disrespect God's image even as you are trying to defend him.

Nobody is won for Jesus Christ at the end of a bullhorn or wagging finger or dismissive or condescending attitude. We can and should engage these questions to help the unbeliever see truth. But ultimately it is the work of the Holy Spirit and not your words that will bring each heart to grace. Make sure that by your words, tone, or actions you don't push that heart further away.

Having said that, here are some abbreviated replies to the above objections. You should have them in mind and frame them with love, not memorize them and unleash them on unsuspecting seekers:

"That's just your truth."

> **Reply:** "Are you saying that it's true that that's my truth?"

"We should be accepting of all beliefs."

> **Reply:** "Why aren't you accepting of my view that your view is incorrect? Can I accept your belief but still think it is wrong?"

"It's arrogant to say that your views are true for everyone."

> **Reply:** "Are you saying that your view should be accepted by everyone? Would it be arrogant to disagree with your view?"

"You shouldn't judge someone else's beliefs."

> **Reply:** "By 'judging' do you mean 'saying another person's belief is incorrect or wrong'? Are you saying that I am wrong to do that? In effect, are you judging my belief?"

[We can't avoid making judgments (John 7:24), but we can avoid judgmentalism (Matthew 7:1)—having a superior attitude toward another.]

"Who are you to impose your morality on others?"

Reply: "I agree. No human should impose a standard of morality on other humans. Or should they? Where exactly does our moral standard come from, if not from humans?"

"You can do whatever you want—just as long as you don't hurt anyone."

Reply: "Are you tacking on a moral rule to your relativistic statement? Why not just say, 'You can do whatever you want—period'? In nature, animals kill each other and we don't judge that. Why are humans different?"

This sliding scale for what is right and what is wrong might seem like a new idea, something that is a problem only in our modern society. But as long as people have been around, they haven't liked being told right from wrong. Just observe a nearby toddler to see that we humans prefer our own satisfaction over that of society or a greater good. Even mature Christians struggle with the things of "self." It's no wonder so many people are attracted to moral relativism: "What is right for you might not be what is right for me." Things get a lot easier that way.

Way back in the fifth century BC, Greek historian Herodotus advanced the view of moral relativism when he observed that different societies have different customs, and that each person thinks his own society's customs are best. But no set of social customs, Herodotus said, is really better or worse than any other.

Some contemporary sociologists and anthropologists have argued along similar lines: that morality, because it is a social product, develops differently within different cultures. Each society develops standards that are used by people within it to distinguish acceptable from unacceptable behavior, and every judgment of right and wrong is according to one or another of these standards. According to these researchers, if practices such as polygamy or infanticide are considered right within a society, then they are right for that society. If the same practices are considered wrong within a different society, then those practices are wrong for that society. In this environment of moral relativism, there is no such thing as what is "really" right, apart from these social codes. According to this theory, there is no culture-neutral standard by which we can determine which society's view is correct. The different social codes are all that exist.

Religious relativism maintains that one religion can be true for one person or culture but not for another. No religion, therefore, is universally or exclusively true. Religious beliefs are simply an accident of birth: If a person grows up in America, chances are good that he or she might become a Christian; if in India, a Hindu; if in Saudi Arabia, a Muslim. If what one believes is purely the product of historical happenstance, the argument goes, no single religious belief can be universally or objectively true.

> "People say, 'Yeah, I'm spiritual. I believe in some kind of god.
> That's good enough. That's fine.' When that's kind of meaningless. If
> you believe in just any god, that means you really believe in nothing."
> LEE STROBEL

"Many people in modern culture take a sort of cafeteria approach to religion. As they go through the line, they pick a little bit of that and a little bit of this and a little bit of that and sort of construct their own religion from these pieces that they pick off the shelf. Now, the presupposition of that approach to religious belief is the modernistic mentality that there is no **objective Truth** about these matters, but that rather religion is just a matter of taste, and therefore, if it tastes good you pick that, if the other part doesn't taste good, you reject that. And because people think religion is a matter of taste or fashion, there's no objective truth here. You're free to just take a sort of cafeteria approach to religious belief."

WILLIAM LANE CRAIG

The Bible is clear about truth. Read the following passages and note your own thoughts about truth.

Jesus answered, "I am the way and the truth and the life. No one comes to the Father except through me." (John 14:6)

....
....
....
....

"Then you will know the truth, and the truth will set you free." (John 8:32)

....
....
....
....

"When he, the Spirit of truth, comes, he will guide you into all the truth. He will not speak on his own; he will speak only what he hears, and he will tell you what is yet to come." (John 16:13)

....

....

....

CHAPTER 14

RIGHT AND WRONG ACROSS CULTURES AND RELIGIONS

Darius was king of Persia for thirty-six years around 500 BC. As he conquered the surrounding lands, he was intrigued by the variety of cultures he found. There is a story told of his conversation with two of these cultures. His observations show the depth of moral relativism.

The Callatians were from northern India and held a practice of eating the bodies of their dead fathers. The Greeks did not do that. Instead they practiced cremation as the right and fitting way to dispose of the dead.

Darius tried to appreciate the differences between the cultures. But when he asked the Greeks in his court if they would ever eat the bodies of their dead fathers, the Greeks were shocked and denied that they would ever do such a thing. Darius then called in some Callatians. While the Greeks looked on and listened, he asked the Callatians if they would ever burn the bodies of their dead fathers. The Callatians were horrified and denied that they would ever do such a thing. Each culture was appalled by the practice of the other.

If you think that moral relativism is a problem of the ancient past, let's hit the fast-forward button.

In 2015 China's Communist Party announced it was abandoning its unpopular "one-child" policy after thirty-five years. However, in China it is still quite common to have "sex-selective abortion."

For centuries, son preference has led to harmful practices toward female babies, ranging from infanticide to neglect of health care and nutrition, often ending in premature mortality. In the 1980s, ultrasound technology became available for diagnostic purposes in many Asian countries, and the opportunity to use this new technology for sex selection was soon exploited. In countries where there is a combination of son preference, a small-family ("one-child" policy) culture, and easy access to sex-selective technologies, serious and unprecedented sex-ratio imbalances have emerged.

In most cultures, the balance between male and female births is about even. However, in 2005 it was estimated the number of Chinese males under the age of twenty exceeded the number of females by around 32 million. There is now clear evidence that sex-selective abortion in China accounts for the overwhelming number of "missing women."[1]

If you think moral relativism is a problem just among those who don't believe in the God of the Bible, let's tackle that too.

The Bible is always a great source of wisdom, and that's true for the conversation about relativism too. In the Bible, we see relativism overtake a culture, and we see the result—in the book of Judges. Here we find God's chosen people, a tribe of the Israelites, doing despicable things. At the end of that whole mess, we see a plain statement on moral relativism:

> In those days there was no king in Israel. Everyone did what was right in his own eyes. (Judges 21:25 ESV)

The Israelites' history with the God who chose them didn't keep them from sliding down the slippery slope of moral relativism—in keeping with the practices of the Canaanite deities. They did what was right in their own eyes. Now remember, this was a people who did have God's Word as their law. They had the Ten Commandments; they knew right from wrong. But they decided their human way was better. Right and wrong for them was relative to their circumstances and desires.

MORAL TRUTH THROUGH GENERAL AND SPECIAL REVELATION

God reveals moral truth through Scripture and through the authoritative teaching and example of Jesus. That is, moral laws are known through **special revelation**. But because all human beings bear the image of God, they can understand moral truths even without Scripture or

---

1   Therese Hesketh, Li Lu, and Zhu Wei Xing, "The Consequences of Son Preference and Sex-Selective Abortion in China and Other Asian Countries," *Canadian Medical Association Journal* 183.12 (Sept. 6, 2011): 1374–77.

without belief in God. This is part of God's **general revelation**. For example, in Amos 1–2, God threatens judgment on nations surrounding Israel for stifling their conscience and doing what they knew shouldn't be done—delivering vulnerable refugees into the hands of their enemies, violating their treaties, and so on. God says that all the world will be held accountable to him and every mouth silenced at the judgment (Romans 3:19). The conscience can be a great help if we are sensitive to it, but we can also resist its promptings so that it becomes "seared as with a hot iron" (1 Timothy 4:2). When it comes to objective moral values, we can readily know that torturing babies for fun is wrong, that kindness is a virtue and not a vice, and that Mother Teresa was morally superior to Adolf Hitler. If a person can't see this, then she hasn't probed deep enough into the foundations of her moral beliefs. The reality of deep evils like rape or molesting children reveal a moral standard we can generally recognize.

General revelation doesn't mean "we can be good without God." Yes, atheists can *know* moral truths, but the deeper issue is one of *being*—how do people come to be moral *beings*? Where does dignity and worth and moral responsibility come from? *Do* humans have special worth? We have no reason to think so if we are the product of blind, deterministic, valueless material processes. This makes sense only if we've been made in the image of a supremely valuable being.

Consider also the following Scripture passages—special revelation—and reflect on how moral relativism shows up or is refuted.

> We all, like sheep, have gone astray, each of us has turned to our own way. (Isaiah 53:6)

....

....

....

....

In those days Israel had no king; everyone did as they saw fit.
(Judges 17:6)

....
....
....
....

Make sure that nobody pays back wrong for wrong, but always
strive to do what is good for each other and for everyone else.
(1 Thessalonians 5:15)

....
....
....
....

How has God revealed to us his standard for right and wrong?

....
....
....
....

There are plenty of situations or circumstances that are not explicitly covered in the Bible under right and wrong. How then do we know what to do? Is there any way to know right and wrong in every situation?

....
....
....
....

Consider the following Scriptures in the context of knowing absolute right and wrong:

He has shown you, O mortal, what is good. And what does the LORD require of you? To act justly and to love mercy and to walk humbly with your God. (Micah 6:8)

"You shall have no other gods before me. You shall not make for yourself an image in the form of anything in heaven above or on the earth beneath or in the waters below. You shall not bow down to them or worship them; for I, the LORD your God, am a jealous God, punishing the children for the sin of the parents to the third and fourth generation of those who hate me, but showing love to a thousand generations of those who love me and keep my commandments.

"You shall not misuse the name of the LORD your God, for the LORD will not hold anyone guiltless who misuses his name.

"Remember the Sabbath day by keeping it holy. Six days you shall labor and do all your work, but the seventh day is a Sabbath to the LORD your God. On it you shall not do any work, neither you, nor your son or your daughter, nor your male or female servant, nor your animals, nor any foreigner residing in your towns. For in six days the LORD made the heavens and the earth, the sea, and all that is in them, but he rested on the seventh day. Therefore the LORD blessed the Sabbath day and made it holy.

"Honor your father and your mother, so that you may live long in the land the LORD your God is giving you. You shall not murder. You shall not commit adultery. You shall not steal. You shall not give false testimony against your neighbor. You shall not covet your neighbor's house. You shall not covet your neighbor's wife, or his male or female servant, his ox or donkey, or anything that belongs to your neighbor." (Exodus 20:3-17)

"Call to me and I will answer you and tell you great and unsearchable things you do not know." (Jeremiah 33:3)

If any of you lacks wisdom, you should ask God, who gives generously to all without finding fault, and it will be given to you. (James 1:5)

Religious relativism, remember, is the theory that there is no objective moral truth. In the video, Paul Copan describes it this way:

"More often than not, people are resistant to the rule of God in their lives. I think that's why relativism is so dominant. People say, 'That's true for you but not for me.' They're not relativists when it comes to what the capital of France is, Paris. They're not relativists when it comes to who won the Super Bowl this past year. They're not relativists when it comes to what the stock numbers are. They're relativists when it comes to God, and they're relativists when it comes to morality."

This quote shines a bright light on what drives relativism—self. If I don't like or agree with what you are saying, I just move the target of truth so that we can both be right. It's easy, it's not confrontational, and neither of us has to make any hard changes.

In what other ways do you think self-centeredness shows up in relativism?

....

....

....

CHAPTER 15

PLURALISM

In many cultures, including modern American culture, relativism often coincides with, or results from, social pluralism. *Social pluralism* is simply the coexistence of diverse people or points of view. Because these diverse worldviews live close to each other, often they are accepted by each other.

In America tolerance is a virtue, and engagement with diversity is even better. Let's be clear, these are both good things. If tolerance requires we coexist but know nothing of each other, social pluralism requires that we actively understand and accept each other. However, this process can sometimes result in the theory that truth is relative—what is true for you is not true for me.

This process can also sometimes result in a watered-down faith system that says all religions are basically the same. This is closely related to relativism and is called *religious pluralism*. Remember the root word, plural, which simply means more than one.

Religious pluralism takes two forms. There's the naive version that states that "all religions are basically the same." The problem with this is that they're not. Some traditional religions believe in God; others don't; and still others maintain that you and I are God. These traditional religions will disagree about the human problem (sin, ignorance, desire) and on the solution to the human problem (redemption, knowledge, extinguishing desire).

To understand religious pluralism, here are a few key points:

a. Traditional religions do not and cannot agree; they simply conflict with one another in many of their basic beliefs.
b. Most religions are attempts to understand and/or engage with Ultimate Reality ("God," "Brahman," etc.).

c. These religions can be vehicles of helping people move from self-centeredness to other-centeredness (this is "salvation" or "liberation").

d. "Saints" in various traditions (e.g., Gandhi, Jesus, the Dalai Lama) show that salvation or liberation is the desired result.

One religious pluralist, John Hick, used the analogy of an earth-centered (geocentric) vs. a sun-centered (heliocentric) perspective, which the Polish astronomer Nicolas Copernicus made famous. Hick said we need a Copernican revolution in theology: rather than a Christian or Jesus-centered view of religion, we should see the Christian faith as one of many religious "planets" orbiting the "sun" (ultimate reality or "God"); no one religion or world religious leader like Jesus can be the vehicle of salvation for all people. That would be arrogant and narrow-minded, perhaps even ignorant or naive, like thinking that the sun orbits the earth.

One problem with Hick's view is that he claimed he had a virtue and an insight that Christians didn't have. The religious pluralist thinks he's right and the Christian is wrong. Of course, if Jesus rose from the dead bodily as an event in history, then religious pluralism would be rendered false.

According to the Bible, both relativism and religious pluralism have gone astray.

There are segments in the Old Testament where the Israelites live in their own highly exclusive community. God brought them out of Egypt under Moses's leadership to live in the desert alone. In that situation, it might seem easy to avoid religious relativism or religious pluralism. Since they were living apart from other cultures, they were not being influenced by other belief systems. But they still lost their way.

Don't feel smug when you think about the Israelites; humbly learn lessons from them (1 Corinthians 10:11–12). We all have hearts that are prone to wander. Even the godly psalmist prays for protection from the wandering he knew all too well:

I seek you with all my heart; do not let me stray from your commands. (Psalm 119:10)

God warns us frequently to hold fast to him and not be influenced by the religions around us:

Do not follow other gods, the gods of the peoples around you. (Deuteronomy 6:14)

Do not follow other gods to serve and worship them; do not arouse my anger with what your hands have made. Then I will not harm you. (Jeremiah 25:6)

Be careful to do everything I have said to you. Do not invoke the names of other gods; do not let them be heard on your lips. (Exodus 23:13)

"You are my witnesses," declares the Lord, "and my servant whom I have chosen, so that you may know and believe me and understand that I am he. Before me no god was formed, nor will there be one after me. (Isaiah 43:10)

If one religion is right, does that make all the others wrong?

....

....

....

....

What does it feel like to say someone else is wrong? What does it feel like to hear that you are wrong? After so many years of our culture embracing relativism, pluralism, and relative truth, how do we start this conversation in our neighborhoods, family, or workplace? Is there any common ground we can start with to walk someone down the road away from relative truth and toward absolute truth?

....

....

....

CHAPTER 16

THE CULTURAL IMPACT OF RELATIVISM AND RELIGIOUS PLURALISM

In a plural culture (where we coexist with people of diverse beliefs and backgrounds) we have a biblical mandate to understand and engage the differences around us. In the same way we are spending time in this study to understand other viewpoints, we should keep the practice going in everyday life. It will help us to have a greater understanding of our own faith and also help us facilitate loving, well-informed conversations that lead to healthy relationships. Coexist? Yes, we should. Adopt relative truth instead of **absolute or objective truth**? No. Let's not.

Used with permission from Tarek Elgawhary, president, The Coexist Foundation.

God calls us to live in this world but not of this world (John 17). That means we can't remain within our Christian "bubbles." We are instructed to make disciples of all nations (Matthew 28:19–20), which means we have to actually get out there, listen to people and understand them, love and relate to them, and after a lot of work doing that, we can usually find a good relational opening to talk to them about the gospel. Evangelism is a process, not an event.

Some individuals and organizations in American culture have taken the mandate of living in the world too far and have lost the concept of absolute truth. They believe in relative truth: yours and mine.

Others have adopted relativism in a completely different way.

You may be aware that there is an ordained pastor in one denomination who has "raised eyebrows" with his relativistic and pluralistic ideas. His name is John Shuck and he says:

> Though I self-identify as a Christian and I am an ordained minister
> in the Presbyterian Church (U.S.A.), I raised eyebrows a few years ago

when I posted an article on my website about how my personal beliefs don't align with those of most Presbyterians.

For example, I believe that . . .

- Religion is a human construct.
- The symbols of faith are products of human cultural evolution.
- Jesus may have been an historical figure, but most of what we know about him is in the form of legend.
- God is a symbol of myth-making and not credible as a supernatural being or force.
- The Bible is a human product as opposed to special revelation from a divine being.
- Human consciousness is the result of natural selection, so there's no afterlife.

In short, I regard the symbols of Christianity from a non-supernatural point of view. And yet, even though I hold those beliefs, I am still a proud minister. But I don't appreciate being told that I'm not truly a Christian.[1]

We can see then, that Americans have decided that not only is truth relative, but they get to be the author and authenticator of their own personal truth. John Shuck has provided a powerful negative example of this. He has decided to redefine what being a Christian and a pastor of the Christian faith means. His approach defies argument. He uses cultural catchphrases like "self-identify" to stake his claim. Anyone who disagrees would be labeled intolerant, ignorant, or worse.

To help us cope with this view and others like it, let's read about proper pastoring:

As I urged you when I went into Macedonia, stay there in Ephesus so that you may command certain people not to teach false doctrines

---

1   Hemant Mehta, "I'm a Presbyterian Minister Who Doesn't Believe in God," *Friendly Atheist,* March 17, 2015, https://friendlyatheist.patheos.com/2015/03/17/im-a-presbyterian-minister-who-doesnt-believe-in-god-2/.

any longer or to devote themselves to myths and endless genealogies. Such things promote controversial speculations rather than advancing God's work—which is by faith. The goal of this command is love, which comes from a pure heart and a good conscience and a sincere faith. Some have departed from these and have turned to meaningless talk. They want to be teachers of the law, but they do not know what they are talking about or what they so confidently affirm. (1 Timothy 1:3–7)

How, specifically from the above passage, are John Shuck and people who share his view missing the mark of Paul's teaching?

....

....

....

....

The Bible reminds us that there is one truth, one right, one way—Jesus.

Jesus answered, "I am the way and the truth and the life. No one comes to the Father except through me." (John 14:6)

Therefore Jesus said again, "Very truly I tell you, I am the gate for the sheep. All who have come before me are thieves and robbers, but the sheep have not listened to them. I am the gate; whoever enters through me will be saved. They will come in and go out, and find pasture." (John 10:7–9)

Jesus is "the stone you builders rejected, which has become the cornerstone." Salvation is found in no one else, for there is no other name under heaven given to mankind by which we must be saved. (Acts 4:11–12)

What do you believe about absolute truth?

....
....
....
....

Is absolute truth an important concept for Christians to discuss? Why or why not?

....
....
....
....

What might be some of the results in a society that doesn't believe in absolute truth or a definition of right and wrong?

....
....
....

CHAPTER 17

IDENTITY AND INTERSECTIONALITY: NEW CONVERSATIONS, OLD IDEAS

American culture has moved in a comparatively short time from the Industrial Age to the Information Age. With the explosion of information came an interesting trend: social. Just look around, everyone and everything is "social." Grandma is on Facebook!

Along this path of change, you may have noticed that Americans have defined themselves differently. Encourage a person to "tell me about yourself," and you will hear quite a different answer than you might have not that long ago. Once a person might define themselves by the roles they play in relationship to each other—"I am a factory worker" or "I am a reporter"— would show the role they play in their community. Or "I am a wife and mother" would show the role they play in the home.

Now you hear us defined by how we understand ourselves and our belief systems apart from our relationships with others. We claim our own identity, stick a flag in it, and wave it vigorously: "I am a proud black man," or "I am a Republican/Democrat," or "I am a Christian/ Muslim/Jew," as if those things tell a person all there is to know about who we are. But they don't. While these things were true of us a hundred years ago, they were not our identity. They were a few of the characteristics that make up our whole, not the whole itself.

As Christians living in a more plural culture, we are wise to understand tolerance.

First, true tolerance is the ability to distinguish between the person and the beliefs the person holds or their secondary characteristics, such as race or political affiliation. It isn't "accepting all views as true" (which is impossible). Rather, it's putting up with beliefs we consider erroneous, false, or just generally disagreeable while accepting people who hold these beliefs as God's image-bearers and among those for whom Christ died.

Please be clear: in order to engage the culture around us, we must understand two things: how much our identity has come to define us, and how much we fear being labeled intolerant. We cling to our identity because we think it establishes or articulates our belief systems. We build a cocoon of like-minded individuals not just for good company but also for validation of *who we are.* Social media encourages this trend by allowing individuals to become isolated in more than one way, allowing only sameness to get close to us emotionally and mentally. Most web-based platforms are programmed to push you to information that you want, defined by artificial intelligence and data collected about what you seem to favor. If you watch hair-styling videos, the software will push you to more content about hair. If you watch neo-Nazi videos, the software will push you to suggestions for similar content.

The social and political climate of our country has exacerbated this isolation trend by encouraging us to build walls around ourselves instead of building the bridges that Jesus built to reach the "other." More than ever, our social and political views dictate who we spend time with, what news channel we watch, what charities we support, even what we do with our free time.

When is the last time you went to a friendly potluck dinner? A block party? Had coffee or lunch with a friend or even picked up the phone to call and talk with your actual voice instead of texting? Now, reality check: When was the last time you watched a 24-hour news channel? Checked social media?

Is this a product of a plural society? Perhaps. Is this a product of our culture accepting relativism? Maybe. Either way, the idea that we can define our own identity is just more of self, and quite contrary to allowing God to define us as he does in these verses:

> But you are a chosen people, a royal priesthood, a holy nation, God's special possession, that you may declare the praises of him who called you out of darkness into his wonderful light. (1 Peter 2:9)

> Now you are the body of Christ, and each one of you is a part of it. (1 Corinthians 12:27)

> So God created mankind in his own image, in the image of God he created them; male and female he created them. (Genesis 1:27)

> He predestined us for adoption to sonship through Jesus Christ, in accordance with his pleasure and will. (Ephesians 1:5)

We do have many facets to who we are, and we should definitely understand ourselves and our beliefs well. But not to define or validate ourselves. We look to our Creator to define us. God has given us our identity and our purpose. People who reject God are seeking to answer those questions in themselves, and this is inherently misguided. Do the actors decide their roles or the playwright? Does the app user change the way the app works? No, only the developer can do that. The creator defines his or her creation. Humans are no different.

Look critically at your own social circle, both on social media and in three-dimensional life. How much diversity do you find? Is your social group more or less diverse than it was half your lifetime ago? Explain:

....

....

....

....

> Let your speech always be gracious, seasoned with salt, so that you
> may know how you ought to answer each person. (Colossians 4:6 ESV)

It can be a great encouragement to see current culture paralleled in the Bible. Of course, people don't really change, and God certainly doesn't change, so it shouldn't surprise us when this happens. But still, let us be humbled when God has the grace to show us a long view of the past that informs the present.

Perhaps you have heard the word *intersectionality* in the news, on awards shows, and even in everyday conversations. Intersectionality is a term that dates back to the 1980s and legal scholar Kimberlé Williams Crenshaw, who noticed specifically that we didn't have an effective way to talk about how the experiences of black women are different from the experiences of black men, and the experiences of black women are different from the experiences of white women. Intersectionality is a term that helps us understand where sexism and racism might intersect. It has been expanded to help us understand that we *all* have several identities that intersect to make us who we are. In some cases, the intersection of those identities can create increased disadvantage. For example, we know that women experience discrimination. We also know that black people experience discrimination. What are the unique ways that *black women* experience discrimination? Or gay Latinos? Or physically disabled individuals who are also poor? In some cases, identities intersect in a way that creates layers of discrimination. Conversely, some identities layer up to create privilege: white, well-educated, wealthy, etc.

What does God have to say to all of this? One place to start is Nehemiah chapter 5, a primer on the Christian definition of social justice. Societal discrimination is at the forefront of the intersectionality conversation, and it is worth reading this chapter (or entire book) in the context of this conversation.

But looking only at Nehemiah for the counsel of God's Word on social justice would be a stunted perspective to take. Isn't the Bible full of intersectionality? And isn't it full of God's favor for those who experience discrimination? Here are some examples:

The lame man in Acts 3 who was also a beggar. Peter heals this man to the glory of God. These identities don't always intersect. You can be born with a disability into a wealthy family—disabled, not poor.

Ruth (the book of Ruth) was a woman, a widow, and a Moabite. She would have experienced social discrimination in the Israelite community with only one of these three identities. Yet the Lord showed her favor first through Boaz and then ultimately by placing her in the lineage of Jesus Christ.

Rahab (Joshua 2:1, 3; 6:17–25; Matthew 1:5; Hebrews 11:31; James 2:25) was a prostitute, a woman, and, like Ruth, a foreigner to the Israelites. These three identities would have caused her great discrimination, yet she too was received into the community of believers, and she too shows up in the lineage of Jesus Christ. God showed her radical and redemptive love.

Zacchaeus (Luke 19:1–10) was a chief tax collector in Jericho (not an Israelite) and was despised by the people. Yet Jesus honors Zacchaeus, inviting himself to stay at his home. Jesus shows grace, and Zacchaeus responds jubilantly.

What does God have to say about intersectionality? The Bible shows us time and time again that God loves all his children. He shows favor to the downtrodden. He lifts up the meek, the weak, the poor, the lame. He elevates those who have no voice in society, the foreigner, those who are despised. God runs to them; he remembers them. It's easy, then, to understand that we who are gospel carriers should run to them too.

How can you live out the gospel informed by the examples of intersectionality that run throughout the Bible? Where are you encountering the weak, the poor, the foreigner, the voiceless, the "other"?

....

....

....

....

Go deeper. How does your own personality intersect to make you feel like you are less loved by God? Victim? Abuser? Broken? Proud?

....

....

....

....

Let the Bible reassure you that in all places where your identity intersects, God runs to you. He loves you there already. This is the hope and the truth of the gospel, and it's as relevant today as it was two thousand years ago.

CHAPTER 18

PROBLEMS WITH RELIGIOUS RELATIVISM AND RELIGIOUS PLURALISM

I. MUTUAL EXCLUSIVITY

Alan Shlemon distills for us the fundamental problem with religious relativism and religious pluralism:

> Different religions have different ideas of what God is like. Some say God is personal, others say God is impersonal. Some say God has a son, others say God does not have a son. Some say God exists in three persons, others say God is a unitarian God. And so they can't all be right. Either God is impersonal or he's personal. Either he has a son or he doesn't have a son. He can't do both when they are mutually contradictory things. And so, different religions have different ideas of what God is like, they can't all be correct. They're either all wrong, or perhaps one is right. But you can't say they're all correct because they contradict each other in fundamental ways.

Review the definitions of moral relativism and religious relativism and explain the difference.

....
....
....
....

Review the definitions of religious relativism and religious pluralism and explain the difference.

....
....
....
....

Review the definitions of cultural pluralism and religious pluralism and explain the difference.

....
....
....
....

Does religious tolerance require us to adopt small parts of each other's religions?

....
....
....
....

What are some ways we can lovingly understand other people and faiths without compromising our own worldview?

....
....
....
....

2. OBJECTIVE VS. SUBJECTIVE TRUTH CLAIMS

"We live in a culture in which we don't make distinctions between objective truth claims and **subjective truth** claims. I definitely have an opinion about my favorite dessert, and I have an opinion about my favorite movie. But there are some things that really aren't based on my opinion at all. I can't change them. You know, 'do I have five fingers or do I have six?' My opinion is not going to change that. Either I have the number that I can count, or I don't. This is an objective truth that's based on this object called my hand, not on my personal opinion about my hand. So I think that that's a situation that we have to distinguish.

"Well, what are the claims about God really? Are they just really an expression of our subjective opinions, like your favorite cookie or your favorite sofa, or your favorite movie? Because if that's the case, there's no point in us getting all fussy about making a case for why I think diet Coke is better than diet Pepsi.

"But the issues related to God's existence are different because they aren't subjective claims. Our opinions can't change whether or not God exists. I can be wrong about God's existence, but my opinion can't change it. That's an objective claim about reality and my subjective opinion has no importance.

"Then we have to ask the question, 'Is Jesus this God?' 'Do we think that Christianity is the true description of the God of the universe?' I can be wrong about this but it's not a matter of my opinion. In the end it either is or it isn't. It's based not in Jim's opinion but in the truth claim that's rooted in the object called Christianity. So, it's an objective claim about God's nature and it can be objectively false. It can also be objectively true."

J. WARNER WALLACE

Reflect on the differences between objective truth claims and subjective truth claims.

....

....

....

COMPASSIONATE CONVERSATIONS

In each chapter, we want to keep an anchor in the core purpose of this study: to equip you with a better understanding of your faith. That's the first priority. As we explore contradicting ideas, we gain a better understanding of the Christian worldview.

As we do that, we may be newly aware of conflicting belief systems in people around us. As you enter into conversations with those beautiful and diverse image-bearers, remember that you can win an argument but miss out on winning the heart. Which would you rather do? I hope you choose winning the heart for Jesus and his kingdom.

In the conversation about religious relativism (my truth, your truth) let's consider two great examples given to us by Paul. One is a statement he makes, another an example he sets.

First, 1 Corinthians 9:19–23:

> Though I am free and belong to no one, I have made myself a slave to everyone, to win as many as possible. To the Jews I became like a Jew, to win the Jews. To those under the law I became like one under the law (though I myself am not under the law), so as to win those under the law. To those not having the law I became like one not having the law (though I am not free from God's law of God but am under Christ's law), so as to win those not having the law. To the weak I became weak, to win the weak. I have become all things to all people so that by all possible means I might save some. I do all this for the sake of the gospel, that I may share in its blessings.

In this statement, how does Paul encourage us to relate to the people of different faiths who are around us?

....

....

....

....

Is Paul watering down the gospel message by adapting his lifestyle to those around him? Why or why not?

....

....

....

....

In Acts chapter 17, Paul is in Athens. Read the passage below (verses 16–34) and underline the places where Paul intentionally relates to the people around him.

> While Paul was waiting for them in Athens, he was greatly distressed to see that the city was full of idols. So he reasoned in the synagogue with both Jews and God-fearing Greeks, as well as in the marketplace day by day with those who happened to be there. A group of Epicurean and Stoic philosophers began to debate with him. Some of them asked, "What is this babbler trying to say?" Others remarked, "He seems to be advocating foreign gods." They said this because Paul was preaching the good news about Jesus and the resurrection. Then they took him and brought him to a meeting of the Areopagus, where they said to him, "May we know what this new teaching is that you are presenting? You are bringing some strange ideas to our ears, and we would like to know what they mean." (All the Athenians and the foreigners who lived there spent their time doing nothing but talking about and listening to the latest ideas.)
>
> Paul then stood up in the meeting of the Areopagus and said: "People of Athens! I see that in every way you are very religious. For

as I walked around and looked carefully at your objects of worship, I even found an altar with this inscription: TO AN UNKNOWN GOD. So you are ignorant of the very thing you worship—and this is what I am going to proclaim to you. The God who made the world and everything in it is the Lord of heaven and earth and does not live in temples built by human hands. And he is not served by human hands, as if he needed anything. Rather he himself gives everyone life and breath and every-thing else. From one man he made all the nations, that they may inhabit the whole earth; and he marked out their appointed times in history and the boundaries of their lands. God did this so that they would seek him and perhaps reach out for him and find him, though he is not far from any one of us. 'For in him we live and move and have our being.' As some of your own poets have said, 'We are his offspring.'

"Therefore since we are God's offspring, we should not think that the divine being is like gold or silver or stone—an image made by human design and skill. In the past God overlooked such ignorance, but now he commands all people everywhere to repent. For he has set a day when he will judge the world with justice by the man he has appointed. He has given proof of this to everyone by raising him from the dead."

When they heard about the resurrection of the dead, some of them sneered, but others said, "We want to hear you again on this subject." At that, Paul left the Council. Some of the people became followers of Paul and believed. Among them was Dionysius, a member of the Areopagus, also a woman named Damaris, and a number of others.

Paul has given two great examples of how to cultivate conversation with those who disagree with or are uninformed about our faith. Share your thoughts on the example Paul sets.

....

....

....

....

As Americans, how do we remain a people who believe in absolutes among a culture that does not?

....

....

....

....

Make a short list of people in your life who might hold the worldview of relativism or religious pluralism. We will come back to this list later with practical resources you can use to engage them in loving conversation. For now, pray for them each day. Ask God to show them evidence of himself in your life, and ask him to show you opportunities to share your faith, with or without words.

....

....

....

....

UNIT 4

THE UNIQUENESS OF CHRISTIANITY

VIDEO NOTES

"We're morally broken people. We're desperately in need of forgiveness and moral rehabilitation."

WILLIAM LANE CRAIG

"Christianity has a solution to our biggest problem that's very different from other solutions."

BRANDON MCGUIRE

"Apart from Christ and his sacrificial death on our behalf, there just isn't anybody else who has paid the penalty for our wrongdoing. There are only two persons who can pay the moral penalty for your wrongs, either you or Jesus. And so, if you reject Jesus and his payment, then there is no one left to pay the penalty but yourself."

WILLIAM LANE CRAIG

"In order to accept the good news, you first have to accept the bad news: that we're broken and we can't fix ourselves . . . and we don't like that."

DONALD WILLIAMS

"So what we see in the biblical story is that there is a God who creates, who makes human beings for relationship with himself. Human beings turn away from this God, but God is not done. Even though there is human rebellion and resistance to him, God is one who is willing to get his hands dirty and to get involved in human affairs, and he is one who is engaging with human beings all along the way. God is saying, 'I am moving toward the fulfillment of what I desire for you,' that is, for God and human beings to dwell in right relationship with each other."

PAUL COPAN

CHAPTER 19

THE FUNDAMENTAL PROBLEM

"This problem isn't just around us, it's also within us."
BRANDON MCGUIRE

Most world religions can agree that this world is not a perfect place. There is a fundamental problem that permeates deep into the human experience. Sickness, sadness, pain, war, death, violence, disease, and suffering show up in every culture, every country, every corner of the earth. Most religions agree this problem isn't just around us; it's also within us. Humans are suffering from this problem and are also the *cause* of this problem. Christians call this problem *sin*.

"In our moral experience as we strive to do the good, we find over and over again that we fall short of the moral ideal, that we act in ways that are selfish, uncompassionate, unloving."
WILLIAM LANE CRAIG

Describe how this quote relates to your own personal experiences.

....

....

....

....

Different religions are responding to different problems, so each religion offers a different solution. For example, Christians identify the problem as sin, and the solution is salvation; for Buddhists the problem is suffering, and the solution is nirvana.

"When you say something like, 'You know what? Islam, Christianity, Judaism, Wiccan, all this stuff . . . it really has the same goal.' Or you know, 'You're all worshiping the same thing,' that belies a lack of understanding, a basic understanding about each of those belief systems because these belief systems adamantly oppose one another with their truth claims."

MARY JO SHARP

CHAPTER 20

WHAT IS CHRISTIANITY AND HOW IS IT UNIQUE?

"You look at many different religious leaders and they would teach methods of getting closer to God. They'd teach rules, they'd teach laws but ultimately it came down to what we needed to do in order to move ourselves toward being better people, move ourselves toward being closer to God.

"Jesus came and did really the opposite. In some ways it was disheartening because the message of Christianity is, 'We all fall short. We can never lift ourselves up by the bootstraps. We can never earn our way.' There's a famous verse that says, 'We all fall short of God's standard' [Romans 3:23: 'For all have sinned and fall short of the glory of God'] and so that's the bad news.

"The good news is Jesus said, 'I came to lay down my life as a ransom.' You think of a ransom, you pay a ransom to free a captive. Well, we were captives to our sin and Jesus did for us what no other religious leader ever did or even claimed to do . . . he made the payment in full."

MARK MITTELBERG

Christianity recognizes that the fundamental problem is within us and goes deeper than even our outward behavior.

A good man brings good things out of the good stored up in his heart, and an evil man brings evil things out of the evil stored up in his heart. For the mouth speaks what the heart is full of. (Luke 6:45)

> Above all else, guard your heart, for everything you do flows from it. (Proverbs 4:23)

> What causes quarrels and what causes fights among you? Is it not this, that your passions are at war within you? (James 4:1 ESV)

Describe how these verses relate to your own personal experience.

....

....

....

....

Christianity recognizes that humans are utterly unable to solve this sin problem on their own. Behavior can be modified by determination, sure. But unless we deal with the heart problem, the old behavior comes back or a new behavior arises. This shows that the underlying problem still exists. For this problem we don't need a system; we need a Savior.

> For all have sinned and fall short of the glory of God, and all are justified freely by his grace through the redemption that came by Christ Jesus. (Romans 3:23–24)

> A person may think their own ways are right, but the Lord weighs the heart. (Proverbs 21:2)

> He knows how we are formed, he remembers that we are dust. (Psalm 103:14)

> For God so loved the world that he gave his one and only Son, that whoever believes in him shall not perish but have eternal life. (John 3:16)

How do these verses impact you personally?

....

....

....

....

Finally, Christianity recognizes that there are two big gifts we gain as a result of the provision God has made through Jesus Christ.

First, we gain our **eternal life**, or life after we die. That means we get to live in heaven when we die not because of what we have done here on earth but because of what Jesus has done for us.

> He will swallow up death forever. The Sovereign LORD will wipe away the tears from all faces; he will remove his people's disgrace from all the earth. The LORD has spoken. In that day they will say, "Surely this is our God; we trusted in him, and he saved us. This is the LORD, we trusted in him; let us rejoice and be glad in his salvation." (Isaiah 25:8–9)

> My Father's house has many rooms; if that were not so, would I have told you that I am going there to prepare a place for you? And if I go and prepare a place for you, I will come back and take you to be with me that you also may be where I am. You know the way to the place where I am going. (John 14:2–4)

The unique marker of Christianity among other religions is the provision of Jesus Christ and him alone for our salvation.

> Salvation is not a reward for the good things we have done, so none of us can boast about it. (Ephesians 2:9 NLT)

The second gift of the provision of Jesus Christ as our Savior is the improvement of our life here on earth, our temporal life. Once we accept the heart change that Jesus is offering, we can live a different life here even before we die.

> The thief comes only to steal and kill and destroy; I have come that they may have life, and have it to the full. (John 10:10)

> I have been crucified with Christ and I no longer live, but Christ lives in me. The life I now live in the body, I live by faith in the Son of God, who loved me and gave himself for me. (Galatians 2:20)

How do these verses impact you personally? Try to share examples from your own experiences.

....

....

....

....

Our ability to create true change in ourselves is made possible only by the provision of Jesus Christ for our heart problem—sin. When we exchange the fundamental problem (sin) for the Fundamental Solution (Jesus), we get an abundant life both here (John 10:10) and in eternity (John 3:16).

CHAPTER 21

THEOLOGY

*T*heology is the study of the nature of God and religious belief. It is a system developed for understanding God. Biblical theology would then be a system of beliefs about God based on the content of the Bible. Biblical theology answers the question: "What can we know about God as he is revealed in the Bible?" There are other ways to know and understand God, but for the purpose of answering the core question of this study, "What is Christianity?" we will focus on biblical theology.

The "five solas" were developed by John Calvin (1509–1564) to offer a structure of basic Christian Protestant theology.

1. **Sola Scriptura** ("Scripture alone"): The Bible alone is our highest authority. The Bible is about Jesus Christ and his role as God and Savior.

   All Scripture is God-breathed and is useful for teaching, rebuking, correcting and training in righteousness, so that the servant of God may be thoroughly equipped for every good work. (2 Timothy 3:16-17)

2. **Sola Fide** ("faith alone"): We are saved through faith alone in Jesus Christ.
3. **Sola Gratia** ("grace alone"): We are saved by the grace of God alone.
   Sola fide and sola gratia express the teaching of Ephesians 2:8:

   For it is by grace you have been saved, through faith—and this is not from yourselves, it is the gift of God—not by works, so that no one can boast. For we are God's handiwork, created in Christ Jesus to do good works, which God prepared in advance for us to do. (Ephesians 2:8-10)

4. ***Solus Christus*** ("Christ alone"): Jesus Christ alone is our Lord, Savior, and King. God has given the ultimate revelation of himself to us by sending Jesus Christ.

> The Son is the image of the invisible God, the firstborn over all creation. (Colossians 1:15)

Only through God's gracious self-revelation in Jesus do we come to a saving and transforming knowledge of God.

> The goal of this command is love, which comes from a pure heart and a good conscience and a sincere faith. (1 Timothy 1:5)

Because God is holy and all humans are sinful and sinners, neither religious rituals nor good works mediate between us and God.

> Salvation is found in no one else, for there is no other name under heaven given to mankind by which we must be saved. (Acts 4:12)

5. ***Soli Deo Gloria*** ("to the glory of God alone"): We live for the glory of God alone. God's glory is the central motivation for salvation, not improving the lives of people— though that is a wonderful by-product. God is not a means to an end—he is the means *and* the end. The goal of all of life is to give glory to God alone:

> Whether you eat or drink or whatever you do, do it all for the glory of God. (1 Corinthians 10:31)

CHAPTER 22

CULTURAL IMPACT OF CHRISTIANITY

You cannot tell the story of America without telling the story of our religious history. While established historic faiths found new life on the North American continent, the United States has also been a place of vigorous invention, continued revelation, and the kind of innovation that comes with liberty. America gathered religions from around the world, was changed by them, and proceeded to change them as well.

Christianity and Judaism are two of these ancient faiths that have flourished in America's religiously diverse democracy. They have also experienced the development of modern American interpretations of what it means to be a Jew and a Christian.

That religious experience in the unique environment of American freedom is part of what drove us to create this study in the first place. We want to explore together the ways we are getting it right and the ways we are getting it wrong here in America.

In 2010 the Pew Forum on Religion and Public Life gave thousands of people a quiz on religious knowledge and religious history. You can still take that quiz online at www.pewforum .org/quiz/u-s-religious-knowledge/ and see how you do. The average respondent got roughly 50 percent right, and of 3,400 test-takers, only eight got all the answers right. That's 0.2 percent.

America has been the home of religious freedom and has a degree of religious tolerance that is hard to find in other places around the world. The question we are grappling with here is whether that freedom has diluted the Christian faith or strengthened it.

Reflect on the impact of America on Christianity and the impact of Christianity on America.

....

....

....

CHAPTER 23

PROBLEMS WITH CHRISTIANITY

You may have noticed by now that there is a structure to each of our units. One of the elements of that structure exists to point out the problems that face each ideology we have examined. Christianity does not get a pass. If we don't understand the problems that the culture has with Christianity, we can't have any hope of speaking into those problems intelligently or thoughtfully. So let's do it. What are the problems with Christianity?

I. THE PROBLEM WITH NEED

"Part of the challenge in our culture with the gospel is even if someone says, 'Yeah, he died on the cross for my sins,' we live, again, in a pluralistic, relativistic culture where a lot of people don't have a great understanding even of what sin is anymore. They don't think they're bad. They don't think they've done anything wrong. So this idea of Jesus dying on the cross, it's just this thought, this idea, it's not an actual fulfillment of a desire."

MICHAEL SHERRARD

"Christ offers us something that we wish we didn't need, which is forgiveness of sin. So that's the sticking point."

DONALD WILLIAMS

The first problem with Christianity is that we wish we didn't *need* a Savior.

2. THE PROBLEM WITH FREE

"We as human beings who are so used to working and striving and performing for love, we have a problem with not being able to contribute something."

—GRANT LEWIS

"There's no such thing as a free lunch."

In a capitalist society, we fundamentally believe you get what you deserve. You work hard, climb out of your social station, and move up. Rags to riches. So when someone presents us with something that is so incredible as to have eternal value, we scoff. It sounds ridiculous.

"If it sounds too good to be true, it probably is."

As humans, but perhaps especially as Americans, it is difficult for us to grasp that we have been given this gift of salvation for free.

3. THE PROBLEM WITH JESUS

"Apart from Christ and his sacrificial death on our behalf, there just isn't anybody else who has paid the penalty for our wrongdoing. There are only two persons who can pay the moral penalty for your wrongs, either you or Jesus. And so, if you reject Jesus and his payment, then there is no one left to pay the penalty but yourself."

—WILLIAM LANE CRAIG

This Jesus problem is pervasive in America. Even if we admit to problem number one, which is that we do need a Savior, we would prefer saving ourselves without any help. American culture is very much committed to the "Pull yourself up by your bootstraps" motto as a means of getting through challenges, and in fact, getting through life. "Shake it off!" and "Dig deep!"

are the battle cries on Little League fields. We learn young to be "self-made" men and women. We esteem the strength of *self*. Flip it around: self-esteem.

If you grew up or raised a child during the 1980s or 1990s, you almost certainly remember the rise of the "self-esteem craze" focusing on how special each individual child is. A certain ethos took hold during this time: it was the job of all involved in the upbringing of children to instill a sense of their own specialness and potential.

The self-esteem craze changed how countless organizations were run, how an entire generation was educated, and how that generation went on to perceive itself (quite favorably). As it turned out, the central claim underlying the trend, that there's a causal relationship

Cornered   by Mike Baldwin

"May I remind you that my core worth as a human being remains constant, and isn't tied to external validation."

between self-esteem and various positive outcomes, was almost certainly inaccurate. But that didn't matter: for millions of people, this was just too good and satisfying a story to check, and that's part of the reason the national focus on self-esteem never fully abated.[1]

This culture shift has created animosity toward the Christian faith and its precepts. As long as we esteem self, we will have trouble laying hold of our need for mercy and grace. Having self-esteem, in and of itself, is not bad. But it becomes bad when a person esteems themselves so highly that they think they are good enough without any help, without any Savior.

4. The Problem with Us

Okay, reality check. Part of the problem with Christianity in America is the delivery system—us. We are imperfect at best and evil at worst. Jesus is used as a weapon, Scriptures as a barbed whip. We misuse and abuse points on theology, religion, and biblical intent. We are hurting people with the gospel. Don't point to your neighbor; I'm talking to you. I'm talking to me. I know your knee-jerk is to point to the "other" on this one, like radical believers we

---

1   Jesse Singal, "How the Self-Esteem Craze Took Over America: And Why the Hype Was Irresistible," *New York Magazine*, May 30, 2017.

see in the media, carrying signs or megaphones to judge and belittle or demean. Don't do it. Be introspective. Ask God to show you how this is happening today in your life. Then fix it.

5. THE PROBLEM WITH THE COST OF DISCIPLESHIP

Many people count the cost of true **discipleship** (following the path of Jesus and allowing him to be your mentor and teacher throughout life) from the outside and decide it's not worth it. This is a perception that all fun is over and Christianity is all rules and regulations, but this couldn't be further from the truth. Following Jesus means having an abundant life . . . life to the fullest. Life without being a slave to society or self. Until you understand the heart-changing experience of the gospel of Jesus Christ, it's hard to understand what truly motivates the life change that is visible from the outside.

Have you experienced any of these problems with Christianity, either in your own journey or in the life of those around you?

....

....

....

....

How can we lovingly address these problems in conversation with those around us?

....

....

....

COMPASSIONATE
CONVERSATIONS

It's not hard to find advice on how to have a good conversation with your neighbor about Christianity. You can look at the "Four Spiritual Laws," which is a small booklet that walks through the principles of the faith and ends with a call to action. You can look at some great work on the Internet and especially on YouTube. Perhaps Christians are a little saturated with interpretations of how to have the gospel conversation. Guess what? God tells us exactly how to do it in the Bible.

> Be wise in the way you act toward outsiders; make the most of every opportunity. Let your conversation be always full of grace, seasoned with salt, so that you may know how to answer everyone. (Colossians 4:5–6)

What are your thoughts on how to live out this verse?

....

....

....

....

God also warns us about false wisdom, even our own. This verse reminds us to rely only on his Word:

For the message of the cross is foolishness to those who are perishing, but to us who are being saved it is the power of God. For it is written:

> "I will destroy the wisdom of the wise;
> the intelligence of the intelligent I will frustrate."

Where is the wise person? Where is the teacher of the law? Where is the philosopher of this age? Has not God made foolish the wisdom of the world? For since in the wisdom of God the world through its wisdom did not know him, God was pleased through the foolishness of what was preached to save those who believe. Jews demand signs and Greeks look for wisdom, but we preach Christ crucified, a stumbling block to Jews and foolishness to Gentiles, but to those whom God has called, both Jews and Greeks, Christ the power of God and the wisdom of God. For the foolishness of God is wiser than human wisdom, and the weakness of God is stronger than human strength. (1 Corinthians 1:18-25)

What are the trappings of human wisdom and how can we avoid them in favor of God's wisdom?

....

....

....

....

Scripture instructs us to meet the people around us where they are, without regard to our own glory by being haughty or "holier than thou," but by making ourselves servants, considering ourselves lower.

Though I am free and belong to no one, I have made myself a slave to everyone, to win as many as possible. To the Jews I became like a Jew, to win the Jews. To those under the law I became like one under the law (though I myself am not under the law), so as to win those under the law. To those not having the law I became like one not having the law (though I am not free from God's law but am under Christ's law), so as to win those not having the law. To the weak I became weak, to win the weak. I have become all things to all people so that by all possible means I might save some. I do all this for the sake of the gospel, that I may share in its blessings. (1 Corinthians 9:19–23)

Do nothing out of selfish ambition or vain conceit. Rather, in humility value others above yourselves. (Philippians 2:3)

What do these verses look like when they are lived out?

....
....
....
....

Make a list of people who have come to mind as you did this unit's work. Pray that God would soften their hearts to the gospel message, showing them the sin that lives in every heart and the beautiful Savior who was provided to solve the problem of sin.

....
....
....
....

WHY THE RESURRECTION MATTERS

VIDEO NOTES

"What distinguishes Christianity, what sets it apart from other world-views, is that there's actually a test by which we can know whether it's true—and that's the resurrection of Jesus."

MIKE LICONA

"The atheist New Testament scholar Gerd Lüdemann says Jesus's execution is an indisputable fact."

LEE STROBEL

"The majority of New Testament historians have come to accept as factual: that [Jesus's] body was interred in a tomb . . . that that tomb was then found empty by a group of Jesus's women disciples on the Sunday morning following the crucifixion . . . that thereafter various individuals and groups of people experienced appearances of Jesus alive after his death. And finally, that the original disciples suddenly and sincerely came to believe, despite every predisposition to the contrary, that God had raised Jesus of Nazareth from the dead."

WILLIAM LANE CRAIG

"How do we interpret the conversions of Paul and James? How do we interpret those four facts that the wide majority of scholars take for granted? How do we interpret that? Do we interpret that naturally or do we interpret that supernaturally?"

PAUL COPAN

"Now, if the resurrection happened, if a man rose from the dead, all of a sudden all of this naturalistic bias goes out the window. There's something more to this world than simply believing that we are one accident after another after another after another that produced life. There's more to this world. . . . That means there's no reason to despair. God can raise you from the dead. That means there's no reason to be without hope because God has worked together, for the good of those who love him, all things. That changes absolutely everything."

NABEEL QURESHI

CHAPTER 24

THE RESURRECTION

Christianity is testable. You can investigate it because at its core it has a certain question that's *investigatable*:

Is the resurrection true?

Reflect now on your own search for truth and your faith in God. Have you walked a journey of emotional connection to Jesus? Of intellectual pursuit of truth? How have you investigated your faith?

....

....

....

....

Jesus foretold his own resurrection on several occasions.

> He then began to teach them that the Son of Man must suffer many things, and be rejected by the elders, the chief priests and the teachers of the law, and that he must be killed and after three days rise again. (Mark 8:31)

When the scribes and Pharisees wanted a sign from him, he said only one sign would be given:

> "For as Jonah was three days and three nights in the belly of a huge fish, so the Son of Man will be three days and three nights in the heart of the earth." (Matthew 12:40)

It is quite risky to foretell your own resurrection. Yet Jesus not only foretold his resurrection but announced precisely *when* he would be resurrected.

Do you believe the resurrection is true? Why or why not?

....

....

....

CHAPTER 25

HISTORICAL FACTS

In order to establish the resurrection as historically accurate, we will use the "Minimal Facts Approach." This four-fact approach is based on the research of Gary Habermas of Liberty University and Mike Licona of the North American Mission Board, both of whom are part of the *Searching for God* videos. This material can be found in their coauthored book *The Case for the Resurrection of Jesus*. Excerpts from Mary Jo Sharp's blog at confidentchristianity.com have also been used, with permission. Mary Jo Sharp also appears in the *Searching for God* videos. Dr. Gary Habermas and others have expanded this argument and added additional facts that are widely accepted by historians (there is one version of the argument that uses six facts and another that uses twelve), but for our purposes here we are going to stick with only the four most indisputable facts because even with just these, there is an incredibly strong historical case to be made for the resurrection of Jesus from the dead.

The "Minimal Facts Approach":

- Looks only at the facts that are supported by multiple ancient sources, both biblical and outside of the Bible.
- Looks only at the facts that are agreed upon by the vast majority of scholars today. The critical scholars can be liberal, skeptical, agnostic, or even atheist, as long as they are specialists in a relevant field of study, such as the New Testament.

FACT ONE: JESUS DIED BY ROMAN CRUCIFIXION

> Then [Pilate] released Barabbas to them. But he had Jesus flogged,
> and handed him over to be crucified. (Matthew 27:26)

> When they came to the place called the Skull, they crucified him there, along with the criminals—one on his right, the other on his left. (Luke 23:33)

In the video, Gary Habermas reminds us that the famous agnostic Bart Ehrman "lists eleven ancient sources for the crucifixion of Jesus." In standard historical scholarly practice, two sources are acceptable to attest to a fact. When it comes to the crucifixion, we have eleven independent sources that attest Jesus was crucified. In terms of historical validation, this is quite exceptional. This incredibly high number of independent sources to a single historical fact puts to rest two points: (1) whether Jesus existed and (2) that he was put to death on a cross.

Take a moment, even as we talk about the "facts," to allow Jesus's death by crucifixion to settle on you anew. Write your heart reflections here.

....

....

....

....

....

....

FACT TWO: THE DISCIPLES BELIEVED THEY SAW JESUS

> Praise be to the God and Father of our Lord Jesus Christ! In his great mercy he has given us new birth into a living hope through the resurrection of Jesus Christ from the dead. (1 Peter 1:3)

> Then he said to Thomas, "Put your finger here; see my hands. Reach out your hand and put it into my side. Stop doubting and believe." Thomas said to him, "My Lord and my God!" Then Jesus told him, "Because you have seen me, you have believed; blessed are those who have not seen and yet have believed." (John 20:27–29)

It is widely accepted by historians that the disciples *believed they saw Jesus.* Of course, skeptics move past this fact to hypothesize *why* the disciples and others believed it (hallucination, body stolen, swoon theory, etc.), but most do acknowledge that the disciples were convinced.

The disciples' belief that Jesus appeared to them is easy to affirm. They said it in the Gospels, they preached it as often as they were allowed, and they died for it.

Paul quotes a creed in 1 Corinthians 15:3–8: "For what I received I passed on to you as of first importance . . ." Though Paul penned these words around twenty years after the crucifixion, he had the knowledge prior to writing the words. This very same knowledge of the appearances of the risen Jesus to the disciples is also found in the writings of the early church fathers, for example, Clement of Rome, Polycarp, Ignatius, Origen, Tertullian, and Eusebius.

It is also worthy to note that the disciples underwent an unusual and profound transformation from individuals who were afraid and hiding to bold witnesses of the resurrection, willing to die to defend what it affirms—Jesus Christ as God.

Skeptics try to offer explanations for what caused this transformation; they do not discern the disciples' accounts as mythology. The disciples would not have been willing to die if the resurrection was a myth that they had made up. So, instead of mythologizing the resurrection, skeptical scholars seek to offer explanations for what these men believed they saw. For example, in *The Psychological Origins of the Resurrection Myth,* Jack Kent attempts to explain the post-crucifixion appearances as grief-induced hallucinations on the part of the disciples.

While explaining this transformation, we must take into account that the disciples were willing to suffer persecution and eventually martyrdom for the man they knew *personally,* including their knowledge of Jesus's claims to be the Son of God and his prediction of his own death and resurrection.

If they knew Jesus's resurrection was a fraud, they would be insane (at best) to die for him, because there was nothing to gain, no political power and no future hope of resurrection for themselves. The disciples faced immense suffering as outcasts in their culture, and ultimately in facing death. Why would they do this for a cause if *they knew it personally not to be true?* Since Jesus claimed to be God and predicted his own death and resurrection, if he was not raised from the dead, the disciples would know he was not raised, and they would know he was a false prophet. Yet they were willing to bear all this. The best explanation of their unusual behavior after Jesus's crucifixion was that they believed they experienced the risen Jesus.

Imagine if Jesus had appeared to you after you had walked with him, learned from him, and watched him die. Write your reflections on this idea.

....

....

....

....

Now consider how the risen Jesus has made himself known to you in your life.

....

....

....

....

Fact Three: Enemy Attestation

Saul was still breathing out murderous threats against the Lord's disciples. He went to the high priest and asked him for letters to the synagogues at Damascus, so that if he found any there who belonged to the Way, whether men or women, he might take them as prisoners to Jerusalem. As he neared Damascus on his journey, suddenly a light from heaven flashed around him. He fell to the ground and heard a voice say to him, "Saul, Saul, why do you persecute me?"

"Who are you, Lord?" Saul asked.

"I am Jesus, whom you are persecuting," he replied. "Now get up and go into the city, and you will be told what you must do."

The men traveling with Saul stood there speechless; they heard the sound but did not see anyone. Saul got up from the ground, but when he opened his eyes he could see nothing. So they led him by the hand into Damascus. For three days he was blind, and did not eat or drink anything. (Acts 9:1-9)

Saul (Paul) was an unlikely convert to Christianity. He had been a known persecutor of Christianity, yet his conversion was based on what he perceived to be an experience of the risen Jesus. His conversion was based on primary evidence (what he experienced for himself), not secondary evidence (such as believing what others told him about Jesus). This testimony carries great weight. Paul's writings in 1 Corinthians 15 are considered some of the earliest writings from the New Testament and are therefore closest to the events themselves. Due to the early nature of these writings, scholars grant much of what Paul reports to be historically probable. What can be shown from this material is:

1. An ardent enemy of Christianity converted to Christianity based on an experience he believed to be the risen Jesus.
2. The convert's name was Paul, and he recorded these experiences himself (a primary source).
3. He testified to the death, burial, and resurrection of Jesus.

Paul also wrote about another foe Jesus appeared to, which was James, Jesus's brother.

> Then he appeared to James, then to all the apostles, and last of all he appeared to me also, as to one abnormally born. (1 Corinthians 15:7–8)

The information regarding James's status as an "enemy" of Christ comes from the reports in the Gospels (Mark and John). This material would not be considered favorable to the cause of Christ by including it in these books. In fact, Jesus's own brother's disbelief in him is a rather embarrassing testimony to the faith. Later, however, James was identified as the leader of the church in Jerusalem—*after* the alleged resurrection of Jesus. He was eventually martyred for his commitment to Christianity, as reported by Josephus, Hegesippus, and Clement of Alexandria. Paul gives an account (above) of the appearance of Jesus to James as part of an early creedal statement in making a defense of the resurrection.

These two men, with nothing to gain materially or politically, with seemingly no other logical reason to do so, began to follow Jesus due to the experiences they had with him after his death and subsequent resurrection. This fact needs to be explained and accounted for, not with mere speculation, but with hypotheses supported by first-century evidence.

Why do you think that Jesus appeared to "foes" and called these previous adversaries to not only follow but proclaim him as Lord and Savior?

....

....

....

....

How does Jesus's appearance to "foes" inform your own conversion experience, if at all? Please reflect on your own experience of being a "foe" to Jesus. There is much to be learned by how we see Jesus call the "foe" to himself.

....

....

....

....

FACT FOUR: JESUS'S TOMB WAS EMPTY

Early on the first day of the week, while it was still dark, Mary Magdalene went to the tomb and saw that the stone had been removed from the entrance. So she came running to Simon Peter and the other disciple, the one Jesus loved, and said, "They have taken the Lord out of the tomb, and we don't know where they have put him!"

So Peter and the other disciple started for the tomb. Both were running, but the other disciple outran Peter and reached the tomb first. He bent over and looked in at the strips of linen lying there but did not go in. Then Simon Peter came along behind him and went straight into the tomb. He saw the strips of linen lying there, as well as the cloth that had been wrapped around Jesus's head. The cloth was still lying in its place, separate from the linen. Finally the other disciple, who had reached the tomb first, also went inside. He saw and believed. (They still did not understand from Scripture that Jesus had to rise from the dead.) Then the disciples went back to where they were staying. (John 20:1–10)

THE JERUSALEM FACTOR

Jesus was crucified in Jerusalem. His empty tomb and his resurrection were proclaimed there first. If Jesus's body had still been in the tomb, why did no one go get the body and drag it through the streets of the city to shut down the Christian movement that had so angered the Jewish officials? This would not be an easy task, but it would be worth getting rid of a blasphemous group of rebels. Furthermore, an occupied tomb would at least have dissuaded enough of the believers to merit some explanation on this matter. However, no apologetic work can be found on an occupied tomb by any of the apostles or even second- or third-century Christian writers: Justin Martyr, Irenaeus, Tertullian, Polycarp, Ignatius, and Origen (to name a few). There is a strong possibility they would have reasoned a defense for an empty tomb, as demonstrated in their reasoning of Jesus's life, death, and resurrection, if they had needed to do so. In addition, no work on the tomb from early Christian opposition can be found, such as Celsus, the second-century Christian critic.

ENEMY ATTESTATION

If testimony about an event or person is given by a source who does not sympathize with the person, message, or cause that benefits from the affirmation, then there is good reason to believe the testimony to be authentic. The empty tomb can be found either implicitly or explicitly stated in the works of Josephus, Justin Martyr's *Dialogue with Trypho*, Tertullian's *On the Spectacles*, and in the Jewish Toledoth (regarded as a derogatory version of Jesus's life in Jewish tradition).

In the Jewish Toledoth:

> On the first day of the week his bold followers came to Queen Helene with the report that he who was slain was truly the Messiah and that he was not in his grave; he had ascended to heaven as he prophesied. Diligent search was made, and he was not found in the grave where he had been buried. A gardener had taken him from the grave and had brought him into his garden and buried him in the sand over which the waters flowed into the garden.[1]

---

1   Alan Humm, "Toledoth," Jewish and Christian Literature, http://jewishchristianlit.com//Topics/JewishJesus/toledoth.html.

In Justin Martyr's *Dialogue with Trypho*:

> You have sent chosen and ordained men throughout all the world to proclaim that a godless and lawless heresy had sprung from one Jesus, a Galilean deceiver, whom we crucified, but his disciples stole him by night from the tomb, where he was laid when unfastened from the cross, and now deceive men by asserting that he has risen from the dead and ascended to heaven.[2]

THE TESTIMONY OF WOMEN

If I had an intention of creating a story to make myself (or my story) look good, I would most likely not include information that would be damaging or embarrassing to the credibility of my story. By that standard, it would be an odd invention to have women as the first witnesses of the empty tomb. Yet, in all four gospel accounts of the empty tomb, the women are exactly that, the first witnesses. This report would be damaging to the case when taken in context of the first-century sociocultural norms. The testimony of a woman was not regarded as highly as the testimony of a man. Habermas and Licona quote a few Jewish writings on this matter:

> The words of Torah should burn rather than be taught to women. (Jerusalem Talmud, Sotah 3:4, 16a)

> But let not the testimony of women be admitted, on account of the levity and boldness of their sex . . . ; since it is probable that they may not speak truth, either out of hope of gain, or fear of punishment. (Josephus, *Antiquities* 4.8.15)

> Any evidence which a woman [gives] is not valid (to offer), also they are not valid to offer. This is equivalent to saying that one who is

---

2   *The Second Apology of Justin for the Christians: Addressed to the Roman Senate*, The Medieval Sourcebook, Fordham University, http://www.fordham.edu/halsall/basis/justin-apology2.html.

Rabbinically accounted a robber is qualified to give the same evidence as a woman. (Babylonian Talmud, Rosh Hashanah 22a)

TESTING THEORIES

With the four minimal facts surrounding the resurrection event, put some skeptic theories to the test. The only possible answer that accounts for all facts is the resurrection of Jesus.	FACT 1: Died by Crucifixion	FACT 2: Appeared to disciples	FACT 3: Appeared to foes	FACT 4: Empty Tomb
Swoon theory: Jesus did not die on the cross, he fainted or swooned and was eventually revived.	✗	✓	✓	✓
Hallucination theory: Disciples have grief-induced hallucinations explaining Jesus' appearances.	✓	✓	✗	✗
Legend theory: Jesus was on man/prophet who died by crucifixion but legends developed about resurrection to convert people to Christianity.	✓	✗	✗	✗
Myth theory: The story of Jesus Christ is a myth that developed much like other ancient religions.	✗	✗	✗	✗
Jesus was resurrected: Jesus died by crucifixion, was buried and subsequently appeared to disciples and others in bodily form.	✓	✓	✓	✓

Which possibility accounts for all of the minimal, agreed upon facts?

Material in diagram courtesy of Mary Jo Sharp at confidentchristianity.com/?p=301.

Why would the gospel writers include women as the number one witnesses to the empty tomb when it would better fit their cause to use men instead? The reason they admit to women as the first eyewitnesses is because they were reporting the truth, embarrassing as that may be.

These three factors contribute to the case for an empty tomb. Though the empty tomb is conceded by 75 percent of scholars who write on the resurrection (versus 95 percent or better on the other three facts), this is still an impressive number for the empty tomb case. The empty tomb is a historically probable event that needs to be explained when discussing the evidence surrounding the resurrection.

In our faith, the empty tomb is a common image to invoke, not just on Resurrection Sunday (Easter) but also through the rest of the year. As you consider the empty tomb today, pause to reflect on it anew. Try to resist the common reflections or ones you have been taught.

Quiet your mind and really consider: What does the empty tomb mean to you?

....

....

....

....

....

COMPASSIONATE CONVERSATIONS

By exploring the evidence around the events of Jesus's life, it becomes surprisingly clear that a resurrected Jesus is the best explanation for the historical facts.

> Now if Christ is proclaimed as raised from the dead, how can some of you say that there is no resurrection of the dead? But if there is no resurrection of the dead, then not even Christ has been raised. And if Christ has not been raised, then our preaching is in vain and your faith is in vain. We are even found to be misrepresenting God, because we testified about God that he raised Christ, whom he did not raise if it is true that the dead are not raised. For if the dead are not raised, not even Christ has been raised. And if Christ has not been raised, your faith is futile and you are still in your sins. Then those also who have fallen asleep in Christ have perished. If in Christ we have hope in this life only, we are of all people most to be pitied. (1 Corinthians 15:12–19 ESV)

"If the resurrection actually happened, it changes everything."
NABEEL QURESHI

We have reiterated several times in this study that conversation must be cultivated with love before facts can become meaningful to a person, no matter how impressive those facts might be. One way to open conversation about the resurrection is to share your own doubts or concerns and how you overcame them. Transparency can be a powerful conversational and relational tool.

Explore ways you can share the miraculous story of the resurrection with your circle of influence (friends, family, neighbors, coworkers)

....

....

....

....

....

This is the last time you will make a list of your friends, family, coworkers, neighbors, and others whom God has brought to mind as you learn about how to engage the culture around you. Pray fervently that he would be at work in those hearts, even now. In the next unit we will reflect on some practical ways to engage the culture, starting with your direct circle of influence.

....

....

....

....

UNIT 6

WHERE DO WE GO FROM HERE?

Video Notes

"Emptiness doesn't come from being weary of pain. Emptiness comes from being weary of pleasure. I don't think there's any statement that describes America today better than that."

CURTIS BOWERS

"The only place where anything in this world makes sense is that spot where the shadow of the cross falls on an empty tomb. Stand there and all questions become answerable."

DONALD WILLIAMS

WHERE DO WE GO FROM HERE?

Except for unit 1, each unit has ended with a section called "Compassionate Conversations." Now we will draw all those skills together for use in real-world situations. View the unit 6 video. It is a compilation of some "man on the street" interviews asking, "What is Christianity?" You may choose to pause after each interview or watch them as a whole. The transcript for each response is below for your use in reflection.

This is a workshop unit, designed to equip you for compassionate conversations about your faith.

Following are some worldviews and cultural challenges we have explored in this study. After each is a quick reference to some of the worldviews we have discussed. Use them as you watch the video. Don't be afraid to note a response with more than one option. The better you can understand each individual's heart on the topic of Christianity, the more equipped you will be to have a good conversation.

After you have identified each response, reflect. Consider discussing these with a friend. Learn from each other. Proverbs 15:22 reminds us that "plans fail for lack of counsel, but with many advisers they succeed."

In the space provided, make notes about what the individual is truly expressing and how to have a loving conversation about Christ's life, death, and resurrection. Please remember that every individual (in the video and in your circle of influence) has an intellectual *and* an emotional response to Christianity. Seek out both with compassion and grace before crafting your response.

Relativism: Religious and ethical truths are unique and valid to any person or culture that holds them. There are no absolute truths.

Religious pluralism: Belief in two or more religious worldviews as being equally valid or acceptable.

Inoculated by Christianity: Having only the understanding that has come from a cultural portrayal of Christianity, possibly resulting in distaste for the perceived image.

Naturalism: Belief in only the natural, denying that any event or object has supernatural significance; specifically the doctrine that scientific laws are adequate to account for all phenomena.

Question: "What Is Christianity?"

Answers:

"It's a religion in which you believe in God and his Son, Jesus Christ, and you go to church, usually every Sunday, and . . . I don't know."

Relativism	Religious Pluralism	Inoculated by Christianity	Naturalism

"Christianity is a . . . my perspective is that . . . what it's done for me and the way I look at it is it's just imposed a bunch of rules and a structure and a hierarchy just as it would be in government or IBM or any other place. It's fueled by money and power and ego. And I don't think that's healthy."

Relativism	Religious Pluralism	Inoculated by Christianity	Naturalism

"I see a lot of greed, I see a lot of hate. I don't see much good coming from it."

Relativism	Religious Pluralism	Inoculated by Christianity	Naturalism

"Our country has been founded on Christianity and just the control of it, and it's not even really about God! It's about control!"

Relativism	Religious Pluralism	Inoculated by Christianity	Naturalism

"It's more of a commercialized industry that. . . . It's a social thing . . . it's a . . . that . . . so many ways to describe it."

Relativism	Religious Pluralism	Inoculated by Christianity	Naturalism

"Christianity is really no different than most religions. There are little parts of the story that are different, but it's the same moral boundaries and whatnot."

Relativism	Religious Pluralism	Inoculated by Christianity	Naturalism

Question: Who Do You Think Jesus Was?

Answers:

"I don't know. A lot of people have faith in him and follow him, but I don't know. I don't spend any time thinking about that. Means a lot to a lot of people, but me, you know, like I said, I stopped thinking about that a long time ago."

Relativism	Religious Pluralism	Inoculated by Christianity	Naturalism

"Some of his teachings and his philosophies coincide with a lot of the other prophets, Buddha . . . you know, all that kind of stuff. And it all goes down to how you treat other people. And if you treat other people right, it's going to come back to you."

Relativism	Religious Pluralism	Inoculated by Christianity	Naturalism

Question: "What Is Christianity?"

Answers:

"Basically, be a good person your whole life, do good to others. You know, the golden rule. It's just common sense. You don't have to be religious to know that. Do good to others like you want to be treated yourself."

Relativism	Religious Pluralism	Inoculated by Christianity	Naturalism

"I don't necessarily think that Christianity is the only way to access God or spirituality." (What would be some other ways?)

"Buddhism, Islam. I think there are plenty of atheists who have access to truth as well."

Relativism	Religious Pluralism	Inoculated by Christianity	Naturalism

"Forgiveness, compassion, grace, faith, belief, and Christianity will teach you those things and will get you there, but it's not the only way. Belief and faith are the ultimate power. Whether you are believing in yourself or you are believing in God or you are believing in another person, belief and faith is really what every single religion teaches you."

Relativism	Religious Pluralism	Inoculated by Christianity	Naturalism

"Basically I think it's possible to achieve a heavenly state, to get to heaven without necessarily needing Jesus's hand."

(Where do you get that idea from, just out of curiosity?)

"That idea? I don't know. I guess that's my own interpretation."

Relativism	Religious Pluralism	Inoculated by Christianity	Naturalism

"You can get there by being a normal person who doesn't have any belief, who doesn't identify with any specific god."

Relativism	Religious Pluralism	Inoculated by Christianity	Naturalism

CHAPTER 26

CULTURAL PERCEPTIONS

For many, if not all, of the above examples you may have included "inoculation" as a descriptor. If you didn't, take a moment to look back on each and see if you can identify it. In the unit 1 video, Tim Keller defines this idea for us by saying,

> "[America is] perhaps the most challenging mission field yet, because no one [has] ever had to evangelize on a large scale a society that used to be Christian. Certainly there have been many times in the past when the church was in serious decline, and revival revitalized the faith and society. But in those times society was still nominally Christian. There hadn't been a wholesale erosion of the very concepts of God and truth and of the basic reliability and wisdom of the Bible. Things are different now.
>
> "Inoculation introduces a mild form of a disease into a body, thereby stimulating the growth of antibodies and rendering the person immune to getting a full-blown version of the sickness. In the same way, post-Christian society contains unique resistance and 'antibodies' against full-blown Christianity. For example, the memory of sustained injustices that flourished under more Christianized Western societies has become an antibody against the gospel. Christianity was big back when blacks had to sit on [sic] the back of the bus and when women were beaten up by men without consequences. We've tried out a Christian society, and it wasn't so hot. Been there. Done that."[1]

---

1   "The Supremacy of Christ and the Gospel in a Postmodern World," Desiring God, 2006 Desiring God National Conference,

When people believe falsehoods about Christianity, it can create a variety of responses, from apathy to strong distaste for the faith. This often causes people to seek out other (in their view more palatable) worldviews like naturalism, relativism, and religious pluralism.

Create some strategies for how individuals and church bodies can begin a conversation by simply correcting the cultural misinterpretations that push people away from Christianity and into other worldviews.

....

....

....

....

....

....

....

....

In each unit you were asked to spend some time in prayer for people in your circle of influence who are holding on to falsehoods about Christianity or holding on to worldviews that are in direct conflict with Christianity. Review those names and prayers now, and in the space provided note how you have seen God at work during the course of this study. Have you had a chance to talk to them, compassionately, about your faith? If not, continue praying that God will prepare their hearts and yours, and that when he sees fit, you will be Spirit filled to engage the culture in your immediate influence.

....

....

....

....

....

....

....

....

www.desiringgod.org/messages/the-supremacy-of-christ-and-the-gospel-in-a-postmodern-world.

As you leave this study, remember to continue to encourage both the believers and nonbelievers in your life. Follow up with them. Pray for them. We engage the culture as a community.

Take heart, friends. The equipping of the Holy Spirit is paramount in the life of every believer. Go forth from this time filled with mercy and grace for the lost, the broken, and the prisoner.

> The Spirit of the Sovereign Lord is on me, because the Lᴏʀᴅ has anointed me to proclaim good news to the poor. He has sent me to bind up the brokenhearted, to proclaim freedom for the captives and release from darkness for the prisoners. (Isaiah 61:1)

LEADER'S GUIDE

The *Searching for God* study guide is structured so that individuals can go through it on their own. However, if you would like to use the study guide within a group setting, this section provides tips and guidance for doing so profitably.

The book is divided into six units, so you may choose to do this as a six-week study with your group. However, there is a great deal of content in each unit. Consider the personality of your group and decide if you want to take more time with the topics. If your group is new to apologetics or is a mix of those who are familiar and unfamiliar with these concepts, it is recommended you take a slower pace.

You will notice in each unit of the leader guide that there are suggestions based on the amount of time you have to spend on each topic.

UNIT 1

THE STATE OF CHRISTIANITY TODAY

Planning

1. Start this unit and every unit by opening in prayer.
2. Collect emails from participants to allow communication outside of the group time.
3. Familiarize the class with the glossary at the back of the book. (All words that are bold and italic appear in the glossary. Please remind participants that this resource is available to them.)
4. This course has a great deal of content. Depending on the format of your class, you may not have time to review all the content as a group. Therefore, you will find suggestions on which material you should, at minimum, try to include. If you have more time, feel free to make a list of secondary discussion points. However, to best equip your small group, try to cover at least those points indicated.

   For this unit, be sure to include the section on worldviews.

   Watch the video after your allotted discussion time.
5. Plan your time for this unit:
   - Plan for as much discussion time prior to watching the video as your format allows.
   - The video is best received after group discussion. Run time of this unit's video is about 10 minutes.

- Plan to leave 10–15 minutes after viewing to discuss the video and wrap up your group time with prayer.
- Fill in your own schedule here:

	START TIME	END TIME
Discussion Time		
View Video		
Discuss Video		

If time is short, focus on these topics/questions:

Imagine for a moment that you are entirely unfamiliar with Christianity. Where in the culture would you find information about Christianity?

....
....
....
....

If the only representation that you had of Christianity is what you saw in the media, what would you "know" about Christianity?

....
....
....
....

How is Christianity portrayed in . . .

- *The Middle* (TV show)?

....
....
....
....

- *The Keepers* (Netflix)?

....
....
....
....

- *The DaVinci Code* (movie)?

....
....
....
....

> "That's the image that, as far as the media is concerned, we present to the public. If that's all I knew about Christianity, I would have absolutely no interest in it."
>
> DR. DONALD WILLIAMS

Reflect on some of the things people associate with Christianity.

- Christianity as one long list of rules or a religious system.

....
....
....
....

- Christians as white Protestant Westerners.

....
....
....
....

- Christians as extremists (intolerant, racist, hateful).

....
....
....
....

List any other descriptions you have heard.

....
....
....
....

Have you ever personally had any misperceptions about Christianity? How have you overcome them?

....
....
....
....

How Do Ideas Become "Worldviews"?

What is your worldview as you start this class? Can you articulate that worldview? If you were asked on the street, "What is Christianity?" what would you say?

....
....
....
....

Reflect on the cultural definition of the following words, and contrast them with the Christian definition of those words. This will highlight how we can "use the same words but not the same dictionary." For help on the Christian definition of each, see the Scriptures noted.

Love

....
....
....
....

Faith

....
....
....
....

Success

....
....
....
....

Do you agree or disagree that modern-day America has been "inoculated" by Christianity? If so, what are some events or moments that have inoculated America, and how do you think this "inoculation" plays out in current culture?

....
....
....
....

Make a short list of people in your life who don't share your Christian worldview. We will come back to this list later with practical resources you can use to engage them in loving conversation. For now, purpose to pray for them each day. Ask God to show them evidence of himself in your life, and ask him to show you opportunities to share your faith, with or without words.

....
....
....
....

If time permits, take a deeper dive into the following areas:

Perceptions of Christianity

How is Christianity portrayed in:

The Middle—The family attends church. In the final season, the mother does expand on "why the hell do I go to church?" when asked by her oldest son.
(www.pluggedin.com/tv-reviews/middle)

....
....
....
....

The Keepers—An extremely disturbing and graphic Netflix documentary detailing the stories of multiple sexual-abuse victims at a Catholic school, victimized by the priests, sometimes as a group.

....
....
....
....

The DaVinci Code—A movie based on the fictional book that many in the American culture accepted as truth. The theory portrayed is that there were multiple gospels and many versions of the life of Jesus.
(www.pluggedin.com/movie-reviews/davincicode)

....
....
....
....

Here are some YouTube clips from the ABC show *The Middle*. Choose one or two to view in class and discuss.

"Church Fires Frankie Up"
    www.youtube.com/watch?v=Vpcjs3TQLLE
"The Hecks Are Late for Church"
    www.youtube.com/watch?v=ZWgoYrnQpB8
"The Hecks Go to Church"
    www.youtube.com/watch?v=zFjXovPqB3c

How Do Ideas Become "Worldviews"?

What are some worldviews that come to mind?

....
....
....
....

In your group discussion, it might seem obvious to talk about other faith systems, and you should. But try to include capitalism and other nonreligious ways we look at the world and make our way through it.

Cultural Christianity

Do you think it's easy to slip out of loving, gentle conversation into arguments about faith and mistaken interpretations or expressions of the Christian faith? If so, what do you think is the cause of that shift in us, and how do we overcome it?

....
....
....
....

Take a moment to talk to your class about the next unit, The Theory of Naturalism. The first unit was conversational, engaging, and interesting, and the video was easy to watch. Unit 2 is a deep dive. Help them shift gears but, most importantly, help them feel ready and able to process the information. Help them to not feel intimidated. Most of all, pray for your small group. You have been chosen to lead them. That extends beyond class time.

UNIT 2

THE THEORY OF
NATURALISM

PLANNING

1. Start this unit and every unit by opening in prayer.
2. Remind the class about the glossary of terms at the back of the book.
3. Do a quick review of the previous unit's material.
4. This course has a great deal of content. Depending on the format of your class, you may not have time to review all the content as a group. Therefore, you will find suggestions on which material you should, at minimum, try to include. If you have more time, feel free to make a list of secondary discussion points. However, to best equip your small group, try to cover at least those points indicated.

   Watch the video after your allotted discussion time.
5. Plan your time for this unit:
   - Plan for as much discussion time prior to watching the video as your format allows.
   - The video is best received after group discussion. Run time of this unit's video is about 13 minutes.
   - Plan to leave 10–15 minutes at the end of class to discuss the video, then wrap up your group time with prayer.

- Fill in your schedule here:

	START TIME	END TIME
Discussion Time		
View Video		
Discuss Video		

If time is short, focus on these topics/questions:

Is the creation of the universe an important question for Christians to discuss with each other? With nonbelievers? Why or why not?

....

....

....

....

What are some examples of mutual exclusivity from everyday life?

....

....

....

....

What are the created things that make you most aware of God's hand? A sunset? The complexity of the human body? The pattern on a leaf or snowflake? Take some time to worship our Creator by listing the ways you see the design of his hand around you.

....

....

....

....

Why do you think that some people can't (or won't) see God in creation? Can you start a conversation about creation and God in a loving, nonconfrontational way by using examples from your list above? If so, how?

....

....

....

....

To review, the theory of naturalism says:

1. There is no God and no supernatural.
2. What we see in our world today is the result of time and chance and the laws of nature working on matter.
3. Miracles are not possible, because they are a violation of the laws of nature.
4. Nonmaterial things such as hopes, plans, behaviors, languages, and logical inferences exist, but they are the result of and determined by material causes.

With this theory in place, other beliefs follow:

1. There is no purpose or meaning to life—we are simply the product of time and chance and the laws of nature.
2. There are no moral absolutes that apply to all people in all times; moral values are simply personal beliefs or opinions, which are the result of chemical and physical processes controlling matter.
3. There is no life after death, for the laws of nature still apply and our bodies simply decay over time and are mixed in with other nonliving matter in the earth.

Looking at the lists above, make some notes about how Christianity offers a different hope, point by point.

....

....

....

....

What are some ways that naturalism has affected American culture?

....

....

....

....

Review the definition of naturalism. What are some ways that naturalism would affect the decision-making process of an individual or society that holds this worldview? In contrast, how does the Christian worldview impact the decision-making process of an individual or society?

....

....

....

....

Do you know anyone who embraces the ideas of naturalism? What snags have you encountered or would you expect to encounter in that conversation?

....

....

....

....

Do you think science and faith contradict each other or complement each other? Why?

....

....

....

....

Make a short list of people in your life who might hold the naturalistic worldview. We will come back to this list later with practical resources you can use to engage them in loving conversation. For now, pray for them each day. Ask God to show them evidence of himself in your life, and ask him to show you opportunities to share your faith, with or without words.

....

....

....

....

If time permits, take a deeper dive into these areas:

What Is Naturalism?

There is a *lot* of content in this unit. Plan your time wisely. Different groups meet for different amounts of time, so don't feel compelled to discuss everything. Choose what you think is right for your group.

Be prepared to manage the group dynamic. This topic can create frustration among believers and even degrade into unloving talk about others specifically or the culture in general. Pray that God will lead you on how to manage that dynamic, but start the conversation by setting boundaries about it dictated by Ephesians 4:29:

> Do not let any unwholesome talk come out of your mouths, but only what is helpful for building others up according to their needs, that it may benefit those who listen.

Reiterate these boundaries as often as needed.

What are some examples of mutual exclusivity from everyday life?

....

....

....

....

The concept of mutual exclusivity comes up later and is important. Take this moment to reinforce the idea with some examples:

> A woman cannot be "a little pregnant." She is either pregnant or she is not; she cannot be both.
>
> When you roll one die, you may get a four or a five, but you cannot get both.
>
> When we flip a coin, we get either a head or a tail, not both.

Consider how much of our culture blindly accepts ideas and theories that Darwin never intended.

The Cultural Impact of Naturalism

Naturalism says that there are no moral absolutes that apply to all people in all times; moral values are simply personal beliefs or opinions, which themselves are the result of chemical and physical processes controlling matter.

The next unit covers relativism and pluralism. Let your group know that these are related to naturalism and perhaps even in some ways an outcropping of naturalism. It's important to help your group begin to see the connection and possibly the chronology of religious relativism and religious pluralism as a result of the rise of naturalism.

Review the definition of naturalism. What are some ways that naturalism would affect the decision-making process of an individual or society that holds this worldview? In contrast, how does the Christian worldview impact the decision-making process of an individual or society?

....

....

....

....

Following the logical conclusion of naturalism leads to selfishness and "survival of the fittest," whereas the Christian faith provides a worldview that promotes love and compassion toward one another through Jesus Christ.

Compassionate Conversations

Your job as leader of this group is to equip the participant with a strong understanding of the state of Christianity today and the major factors or worldviews that are in conflict. However, with strong understanding can often come strong feelings that sometimes lead to strong arguments. Help your participants be grace filled in their conversations—both inside the group and outside of it. We have all been lost at some time. Grace and mercy are all that save us from our own lost ways, and grace and mercy are the only ways to win a heart. Compassion is the key to productive conversation.

UNIT 3

THE THEORY OF RELATIVISM

PLANNING

1. Start this unit and every unit by opening in prayer.
2. Remind the class about the glossary of terms at the back of the book.
3. Do a quick review of the previous unit's material.
4. This course has a great deal of content. Depending on the format of your class, you may not have time to review all the content as a group. Therefore, you will find suggestions on which material you should, at minimum, try to include. If you have more time, feel free to make a list of secondary discussion points. To best equip your small group, try to cover at least those points indicated.

   Watch the video after your allotted discussion time.
5. Plan your time for this unit:
   - Plan for as much discussion time prior to watching the video as your format allows.
   - The video is best received after group discussion. Run time of this unit's video is about 8 minutes.

- Plan to leave 10–15 minutes at the end of class to discuss the video and wrap up your group time with prayer.
- Fill in your schedule here:

	START TIME	END TIME
Discussion Time		
View Video		
Discuss Video		

If time is short, focus on these topics/questions:

What are some other ideas that are relative? What are some ideas that are *not* relative?

....
....
....
....

There are plenty of situations or circumstances that are not explicitly covered in the Bible under right and wrong. How then do we know what to do? Is there any way to know right and wrong in every situation?

....
....
....
....

If one religion is right, does that make all the others wrong?

....
....
....
....

What does it feel like to say someone else is wrong? What does it feel like to hear that you are wrong? After so many years of our culture embracing relativism, pluralism, and relative truth, how do we start this conversation in our neighborhoods, family, or

workplace? Is there any common ground we can start with to walk someone down the road away from relative truth and toward absolute truth?

....

....

....

....

What might be some of the results in a society that doesn't believe in absolute truth or a definition of right and wrong?

....

....

....

....

What are some ways we can lovingly understand other people/faiths without compromising our own worldview?

....

....

....

....

Reflect on the differences between objective truth claims and subjective truth claims.

....

....

....

....

Is Paul watering down the gospel message by adapting his lifestyle to those around him? Why or why not?

....

....

....

....

Paul has given two great examples of how to cultivate conversation with those who disagree with or are uninformed about our faith. Share your thoughts on the example Paul sets.

....

....

....

....

As Americans, how do we remain a people who believe in absolutes in a culture that does not?

....

....

....

....

If time permits, take a deeper dive into these areas:

What Is Relativism?

What are some ideas that are relative? What are some ideas that are *not* relative?

....

....

....

....

Some things are in fact relative, and some are not. For example, what side of the road we drive on is relative to the country where we are driving.

Wedding traditions are relative. Can the groom see the bride before the ceremony? What color should the bride wear? In China the bride wears red. White is traditionally worn for funerals in China.

Food taste is relative; some like cilantro, some don't.

Women's pants size is relative. US size 6 is Europe size 34.

What nonreligious facts are not relative?

2 + 2 = 4, laws of gravity, etc.

How has God revealed to us his standard for right and wrong?

....

....

....

....

The authority for the Christian worldview is the Bible. Discuss with your group the importance of God's Word, especially in response to this question.

> "Call to me and I will answer you and tell you great and unsearchable things you do not know." (Jeremiah 33:3)

> If any of you lacks wisdom, you should ask God, who gives generously to all without finding fault, and it will be given to you. (James 1:5)

These verses on wisdom are pertinent in the context of right and wrong as we attempt to discern those situations and circumstances that are not explicitly laid out in Scripture.

In what other ways do you think self-centeredness shows up in relativism?

....

....

....

....

In her book *The Hiding Place*, Corrie ten Boom explores right and wrong in the context of the Nazi occupation of the Netherlands. The book unpacks, from Corrie's firsthand perspective, the role of faith in situational ethics. This book is strongly recommended for further reading on both topics.

Pluralism

Plan your group time on the difference between social pluralism and religious pluralism. Stress the importance of social pluralism and how that allows diverse people groups to coexist. Also stress the importance of how religious pluralism is in direct conflict with Christianity.

Religious pluralism: In a video excerpt from CBS, Bob Schieffer comments on religions and the common thread through all of them—love. A nice thought and a classic example of religious pluralism (www.youtube.com/watch?v=2UB6fZoXDDo). Or find this clip via YouTube Search: "Bob Schieffer All Religions Share One Truth."

What does it feel like to say someone else is wrong? What does it feel like to hear that you are wrong? After so many years of our culture embracing relativism, pluralism, and relative truth, how do we start this conversation in our neighborhoods, family, and workplace? Is there any common ground we can start with to walk someone down the road away from relative truth and toward absolute truth?

....

....

....

....

If you don't feel good in a conversation, and the other person doesn't feel good in the conversation, what then? Press in with your group on this topic. Help them find their own way to deal with the discomfort that results from embracing absolute truth.

Problems with Religious Relativism and Religious Pluralism

Review the definitions of moral relativism and religious relativism and explain the difference.

....

....

....

....

These definitions are found in the glossary for quick reference in class.

Compassionate Conversation

Paul has given two great examples of how to cultivate conversation with those who disagree with or are uninformed about our faith. Share your thoughts on the examples Paul set.

....

....

....

....

Encourage your group to think about what Paul's examples might look like in present-day American culture.

UNIT 4

THE UNIQUENESS
OF CHRISTIANITY

PLANNING

1. Start this unit and every unit by opening in prayer.
2. Remind the class about the glossary of terms at the back of the book.
3. Do a quick review of the previous unit's material.
4. Depending on the format of your class, you may not have time to review all the content as a group. The questions and discussion points highlighted in blue are suggested material you should, at a minimum, try to include. If you have more time, make a list of secondary discussion points.

    Watch the video after your discussion time.
5. Plan your time for this unit:
    - Plan for as much discussion time prior to watching the video as your format allows.
    - The video is best received after group discussion. Run time of this unit's video is about 10 minutes.
    - Leave 10–15 minutes at the end of class to discuss the video and wrap up your group time with prayer.

- Fill in your schedule here:

	START TIME	END TIME
Discussion Time		
View Video		
Discuss Video		

If time is short, focus on these topics/questions:

> For all have sinned and fall short of the glory of God, and all are justified freely by his grace through the redemption that came by Christ Jesus. (Romans 3:23–24)

> A person may think their own ways are right, but the LORD weighs the heart. (Proverbs 21:2)

> He knows how we are formed, he remembers that we are dust. (Psalm 103:14)

> For God so loved the world that he gave his one and only Son, that whoever believes in him should not perish but have eternal life. (John 3:16)

How do these verses impact you personally?

....

....

....

....

> [The LORD] will swallow up death forever. The Sovereign LORD will wipe away the tears from all faces; he will remove his people's disgrace from all the earth. The LORD has spoken. In that day they will say, "Surely this is our God; we trusted in him, and he saved us. This is

the LORD, we trusted in him; let us rejoice and be glad in his salvation."
(Isaiah 25:8-9)

My Father's house has many rooms; if that were not so, would I
have told you that I am going there to prepare a place for you? And if
I go and prepare a place for you, I will come back and take you to be
with me that you also may be where I am. You know the way to the
place where I am going. (John 14:2-4)

For by grace you have been saved through faith. And this is not
your own doing; it is the gift of God, not a result of works, so that no
one may boast. (Ephesians 2:8-9 ESV)

The thief comes only to steal and kill and destroy; I have come that
they may have life, and have it to the full. (John 10:10)

I have been crucified with Christ and I no longer live, but Christ
lives in me. The life I now live in the body, I live by faith in the Son of
God, who loved me and gave himself for me. (Galatians 2:20)

How do these verses impact you personally? Try to share examples from your own life and experiences.

....

....

....

....

Reflect on the impact of America on Christianity and the impact of Christianity on America.

....

....

....

....

If time permits, take a deeper dive into these areas:

The Fundamental Problem

> "When you say something like, 'You know what? Islam, Christianity, Judaism, Wiccan, all this stuff . . . it really has the same goal.' Or, you know, 'You're all worshiping the same thing,' that belies a lack of understanding, a basic understanding about each of those belief systems because these belief systems adamantly oppose one another with their truth claims."
>
> MARY JO SHARP

You might want to remind participants that the way that these truth claims oppose each other is called "mutual exclusivity." Remind them of the exercise where you looked at other examples of mutually exclusive facts or events.

UNIT 5

WHY THE RESURRECTION MATTERS

PLANNING

1. Start this unit and every unit by opening in prayer.
2. Remind the class about the glossary of terms at the back of the book.
3. Do a quick review of the previous unit's material.
4. Depending on the format of your class, you may not have time to review all the content as a group. Try to include, at a minimum, the questions and discussion points highlighted in blue. If you have more time, make a list of secondary discussion points. To best equip your small group, try to cover at least those points highlighted in blue.

   Watch the video after your allotted discussion time.
5. Plan your time for this unit:
   - Plan for as much discussion time prior to watching the video as your format allows.
   - The video is best received after group discussion. Run time of this unit's video is about 13 minutes.
   - Plan to leave 10–15 minutes at the end of class to discuss the video and wrap up your group time with prayer.

- Fill in your schedule here:

	START TIME	END TIME
Discussion Time		
View Video		
Discuss Video		

If time is short, focus on these topics/questions.

How does Jesus's appearance to "foes" inform your own conversion experience, if at all? Please reflect on your own experience of being a "foe" to Jesus. There is much to be learned by how we see Jesus call the "foe" to himself.

....
....
....
....

In our faith, the empty tomb is a common image to invoke, not just on Resurrection Sunday (Easter), but also through the rest of the year. As you consider the empty tomb today, pause to reflect on it anew. Try to resist the common reflections or ones you have been taught. Quiet your mind and really consider: What does the empty tomb mean to you?

....
....
....
....

Explore ways you can share the miraculous story of the resurrection with your circle of influence (friends, family, neighbors, coworkers).

....
....
....

UNIT 6

WHERE DO WE GO FROM HERE?

PLANNING

1. Start this unit and every unit by opening in prayer.
2. Remind the class about the glossary of terms at the back of the book.
3. Do a quick review of the previous unit's material.
4. Plan to watch the video twice during class. Watch it once all the way through so the group can take in the entire message. Then, watch it again as you read through the workshop on the following pages, using the video as a tool. Try to complete the entire workshop during class time.
5. Plan your time for this unit:
   - Plan for as much discussion time prior to watching the video as your format allows.
   - The video is best received after group discussion. Run time of this unit's video is about 8 minutes.

     The end of this video segment is inspiring and encouraging. Perhaps during the workshop, pause after the last "man on the street" interview to have your group conversation. Then, just before you pray and finish the course, play again the apologetic scholar's summary about our faith at the end of the video.

- Fill in your schedule here:

	START TIME	END TIME
Discussion Time		
View Video		
Discuss Video		

If time is short, focus on these topics/questions:

Create some strategies for how individuals and church bodies can start a conversation with someone by simply correcting the cultural misinterpretations that push people away from Christianity and into other worldviews.

....

....

....

....

Discuss the workshop questions and responses. What other questions and talking points would keep a conversation going?

....

....

....

....

What Is Christianity?

Answer: "It's a religion in which you believe in God and his Son Jesus Christ and you go to church, usually every Sunday, and . . . I don't know."

This answer shows the individual has been inoculated by Christianity. He has only a peripheral understanding of the faith. Interestingly, he is not showing distaste, but definitely confusion that is found in that "cultural only" understanding.

What would you ask next?

....

....

....

....

Answer: "Christianity is a . . . my perspective is that . . . what it's done for me and the way I look at it is it's just imposed a bunch of rules and a structure and a hierarchy just as it would be in government or IBM or any other place. It's fueled by money and power and ego. And I don't think that's healthy."

This response is interesting, because he shows some strong distaste for his perception of Christianity. Inoculation would be applicable here, but since he referenced other social structures, perhaps a touch of pluralism is in there too. He may think that Christianity is the same as other nonreligious social structures, like government.

What would you ask next?

....

....

....

....

Answer: "I see a lot of greed, I see a lot of hate. I don't see much good coming from it."

This is an inoculated response. This person shows some familiarity for the "church" but believes that only bad things come from the church.

What would you ask next?

....

....

....

....

Answer: "Our country has been founded on Christianity and just the control of it and it's not even really about God! It's about control!"

This is an inoculated response. She seems to have an idea of what Christianity is, or at least she thinks she does. She clearly doesn't want to be controlled; she says that word twice. Something in her life connected a bad kind of control (after all, control of your car while driving is a good thing) with Christianity.

What would you ask next?

....

....

....

....

Answer: "It's more of a commercialized industry that. . . . It's a social thing . . . it's a . . . that . . . so many ways to describe it."

This man gives an interesting response that reminds us conversations are dynamic. Classifying these responses into categories we have defined can be helpful. But not all replies will be easy to classify. To equate Christianity with corporate entities is an interesting way to look at it. He then says maybe Christianity is a social construct, as if it were developed from a need for community. He has some ideas on what Christianity looks like. He seems to focus on the corporate aspect and not the individual aspect of Christianity.

What would you ask next?

....

....

....

....

Answer: "It's really no different than most religions. There are little parts of the story that are different, but it's the same moral boundaries and whatnot."

This is classic religious pluralism. The first part of this statement could not be more clear. This person thinks all religions are the same.

What would you ask next?

....

....

....

....

Who Do You Think Jesus Was?

Answer: "I don't know. A lot of people have faith in him and follow him, but I don't know. I don't spend any time thinking about that. Means a lot to a lot of people, but me, you know, like I said, I stopped thinking about that a long time ago."

This response shows inoculation and an apathy toward Christianity. This might be the saddest of all the replies, because at least some of the others are seeking truth. This man seems to have given up.

What would you ask next?

....

....

....

....

Answer: "Some of his teachings and his philosophies coincide with a lot of the other prophets, Buddha . . . you know, all that kind of stuff. And it all goes down to how you treat other people. And if you treat other people right, it's going to come back to you."

This reply is classic religious pluralism. This man believes that Christianity is the same as other religions and dismisses all religions as a group. He asserts instead the common attitude that following the golden rule will be your ticket to a good life here on earth.

He doesn't mention afterlife or whether he thinks it will work for heaven too, but that would be a question to pose if you were in conversation with him. Often when an individual dismisses religion altogether, he/she embraces naturalism. Only gentle, grace-filled conversation can draw that out.

What would you ask next?

....

....

....

....

What Is Christianity?

Answer: "Basically be a good person your whole life, do good to others. You know, the golden rule. It's just common sense. You don't have to be religious to know that. Do good to others like you want to be treated yourself."

This response is similar to the previous response, asserting that the golden rule is good enough. He dismisses religion, which could be an indicator of naturalism, but one would have to press in to the conversation a bit to see.

What would you ask next?

....

....

....

....

Answer: "I don't necessarily think that Christianity is the only way to access God or spirituality.

(What would be some other ways?)

"Buddhism, Islam. I think there are plenty of atheists who have access to truth as well."

The beginning of this comment is classic religious pluralism. However, she throws a curve ball at the end there with the idea that "atheists have access to truth as well." This probably would indicate a naturalistic perspective, but in combination with the prior statement about how to access God, it's a bit contradictory. If she believes there is a God to access via whatever means, then does she believe that God is not truth? Or, if God is truth, how would an atheist "access" that? Here again, you can see that more conversation is needed.

What would you ask next?

....
....
....
....

Answer: "Forgiveness, compassion, grace, faith, belief, and Christianity will teach you those things and will get you there, but it's not the only way. Belief and faith are the ultimate power. Whether you are believing in yourself or you are believing in God or you are believing in another person, belief and faith are really what every single religion teaches you."

This young woman gets off to a great start by using many words we understand as Christian precepts. However, she moves quickly into religious pluralism. She does indicate that she thinks all religions are the same. However, she also says some interesting things about self that could indicate she doesn't believe in God at all. More conversation is needed to unpack what she personally believes. Some of her phrasing indicates her statements on faith might be observations of the culture around her and not necessarily her own viewpoints.

What would you ask next?

....
....
....
....

Answer: "Basically, I think it's possible to achieve a heavenly state, to get to heaven without necessarily needing Jesus's hand.

(Where do you get that idea from, just out of curiosity?)

"That idea? I don't know. I guess that's my own interpretation."

This answer is great, because you can see how this young man begins to understand that his argument falls apart under the smallest bit of scrutiny. The interviewer did not ask a confrontational question to draw that out. Rather, he just asked the young man to examine a bit for himself. This answer, by the way, is closest to religious pluralism, but could also indicate relativism.

What would you ask next?

....

....

....

....

Answer: "You can get there by being a normal person who doesn't have any belief, who doesn't identify with any specific god."

This response could indicate relativism or naturalism. It depends on what she means by "get there."

What would you ask next?

....

....

....

....

You may find that many of these answers indicate a lack of desire to look too closely at the foundation they are built on. This is quite characteristic of the layperson who follows the thought of "that's true for you but not for me" or "all religions are the same." Sure, the scholars can argue back and forth quite well. But most average people, the folks you will be blessed with in your journey, will not have a well-formed foundation for their sound bite. If you do have a solid foundation for your beliefs, and hopefully this course has helped you there, you just might be able to help them examine their beliefs and find reason to believe in Jesus!

GLOSSARY
OF TERMS

Some definitions are taken from Merriam-Webster's dictionary. Other definitions here are for complex words or concepts used in the video and/or the course.

absolute truth: A belief or claim that matches up with reality. Absolute (or objective) truth is not based on human opinion, preference, or culture; it is true independent of them.

biblical worldview: Beliefs anchored in the Bible as God's inspired Word and in Jesus as God's unique revelation to us.

Big Bang theory: Theory that states the universe originated billions of years ago in an explosion from a single point of nearly infinite energy density.

co-regent: One of two rulers who share responsibility for governing a kingdom; in this case, we are co-regents with God who are responsible for caring for the earth.

cultural Christianity: Cultural Christianity is religion that superficially identifies itself as "Christianity" but does not truly adhere to the faith. A "cultural Christian" is a nominal believer: he wears the label "Christian," but the label has more to do with his family background and upbringing than any personal conviction that Jesus is Lord. Cultural Christianity is more social than spiritual.

discipleship: Following the path of Jesus and allowing him to be your mentor and teacher throughout life.

eternal life: A supernatural quality of life bestowed by God's Spirit that begins now and continues everlastingly (cf. John 17:3; modified from Merriam-Webster).

evolution: Charles Darwin's theory that different kinds of living organisms have developed and diversified from earlier forms during the history of the earth.

inoculated by Christianity: Having only the understanding that has come from a cultural portrayal of Christianity, possibly resulting in distaste for the perceived image.

intelligent design: The theory that life or the universe cannot have arisen by chance and was designed and created by some intelligent entity.

intersectionality: The interconnected nature of social categorizations such as race, class, and gender as they apply to a given individual or group, regarded as creating overlapping and interdependent systems of discrimination or disadvantage.

miracle: A surprising and welcome event that is not explicable by natural or scientific laws and is therefore considered to be the work of a divine agency.

mutual exclusivity: Being related such that each excludes or precludes the other.

natural selection: Process whereby organisms better adapted to their environment tend to survive and produce more offspring; theorized by Charles Darwin.

naturalism: A theory denying that an event or object has a supernatural significance; specifically, the doctrine that scientific laws are adequate to account for all phenomena. (Note the threefold characteristics cited in the study guide—materialism, determinism, and scientism.)

objective truth: A claim based on reality, not a personal opinion or preference (modified from Merriam-Webster).

relativism: (a) A theory that knowledge is relative to the limited nature of the mind and the conditions of knowing. (b) A view that ethical truths depend on the individuals and groups holding them.

religious pluralism: The belief in two or more religious worldviews as being equally valid or acceptable and capable of saving or liberating.

sin: An immoral thought, attitude, or act considered to be a transgression against God's character and divine law.

social Darwinism: Herbert Spencer's theory that human groups and races are subject to the same laws of natural selection as Charles Darwin had perceived in plants and animals in nature.

social pluralism: A state of society in which members of diverse ethnic, racial, religious, or social groups maintain and develop their traditional culture or special interest within the confines of a common civilization.

soteriology: The study of the doctrine of salvation.

soul: The spiritual or immaterial part of a human being, regarded as immortal.

subjective truth: A claim based on a personal opinion or feeling.

supernatural: Of or relating to an order of existence beyond the visible observable universe; especially of or relating to God or a god, demigod, spirit, or devil.

theism: Belief in the existence of a god or gods, *specifically* the belief in the existence of one God viewed as the creative source of the human race and the world, and who is transcendent yet immanent in the world.

theist: A person who believes in the existence of a god or gods. See **theism.**

theology: The study of the nature of God and religious belief.

worldview: A comprehensive conception or apprehension of the world, especially from a specific standpoint.

RECOMMENDED FOR FURTHER READING

Each of the *Searching for God* collaborators has authored at least one great book on Christian apologetics. They all stand strong as additional sources for your journey into the faith.

Paul Copan, *Is God a Moral Monster?: Making Sense of the Old Testament God*

William Lane Craig, *Reasonable Faith: Christian Truth and Apologetics*

Gary R. Habermas, *The Historical Jesus: Ancient Evidence for the Life of Christ*

Craig J. Hazen, *Five Sacred Crossings: A Novel*

Michael R. Licona, *The Resurrection of Jesus: A New Historiographical Approach*

Mark Mittelberg, *Choosing Your Faith: In a World of Spiritual Options*

Nabeel Qureshi (RZIM), *Seeking Allah, Finding Jesus: A Devout Muslim Encounters Christianity*

Mary Jo Sharp, *Why Do You Believe That?*

Michael Sherrard, *Relational Apologetics*

Alan Shlemon, *Stand to Reason*

John Stonestreet, with W. Gary Phillips and William E. Brown, *Making Sense of Your World: A Biblical Worldview*

Lee Strobel, *The Case for Christ: A Journalist's Personal Investigation of the Evidence for Jesus*

J. Warner Wallace, *Cold-Case Christianity: A Homicide Detective Investigates the Claims of the Gospels*

Donald Williams, *Mere Humanity: G. K. Chesterton, C. S. Lewis, and J. R. R. Tolkien on the Human Condition*